# FONdA SAN MIGUEL

## Forty Years of Food and Art

New Edition

TOM GILLILAND AND MIGUEL RAVAGO

Foreword by Robert Rodriguez

UNIVERSITY OF TEXAS PRESS, AUSTIN

Copyright © 2005, 2016 by Cuisines de Mexico, Inc.

Copyright © 2016 by TM Photo Inc.

Printed in China

First edition, 2005

New edition, 2016

Requests for permission to reproduce material from this work should be sent to:
    Permissions
    University of Texas Press
    P.O. Box 7819
    Austin, TX 78713-7819
    http://utpress.utexas.edu/index.php/rp-form

♾ The paper used in this book meets the minimum requirements of ANSI/NISO Z39.48-1992 (R1997) (Permanence of Paper).

Library of Congress Cataloging-in-Publication Data

Names: Gilliland, Tom, 1938– author. | Ravago, Miguel, author.
    | Rodriguez, Robert, 1968– writer of supplementary textual content.
Title: Fonda San Miguel : forty years of food and art /
    Tom Gilliland and Miguel Ravago ; foreword by
    Robert Rodriguez.
Description: New edition. | Austin : University of Texas Press,
    2016. | Includes index.
Identifiers: LCCN 2016008493 | ISBN 978-1-4773-1022-9
    (cloth : alk. paper)
Subjects: LCSH: Cooking, Mexican. | Fonda San Miguel. |
    LCGFT: Cookbooks. Classification: LCC TX716.M4 G54
    2016 | DDC 641.5972--dc23
LC record available at http://lccn.loc.gov/2016008493

Recipe for Bolillos (page 175) reprinted with the permission of Simon & Schuster Adult Publishing Group from *Cocina de la Familia* by Marilyn Tausend. Copyright © 1997 by Marilyn Tausend.

To the special women
in our lives,
Amelia Velásquez Galbraith
and Elizabeth Gilliland

*M.R.*

*T.G.*

# Contents

## A NOTE TO THE COOK

The following symbols are used in the recipes:

❁ Indicates a recipe inspired by Diana Kennedy.

❖ Refers to a separate section explaining how to make basic components of various dishes. See "Basic Preparations," page 219.

✿ Refers to a separate section on working with special ingredients. See "Unique Ingredients and Techniques," page 222.

# Foreword

Let's talk about passion.

If you're checking out this book, chances are you know the cuisine already and have eaten at Fonda San Miguel, so I'm preaching to the choir. And if you've eaten there, you've probably seen me sitting in the main dining room by the window. Or maybe you didn't really see me, but that would be because my face was buried in my plate.

But let's talk about passion.

Tom and Miguel are as passionate about the food and the ambience as they are about family and friends. Their food is some of the greatest and most authentic interior Mexican cuisine ever offered up in a stateside restaurant.

I remember when I first introduced filmmaker Guillermo del Toro to Fonda, where he said he hadn't eaten some of those classic dishes since his grandmother made them. Francis Ford Coppola fell instantly in love when I brought him to the Sunday brunch. Bruce Willis called me once out of the blue and asked, "What was the name of that restaurant again that you took us to?" I could hear him smiling on the other end, because he was still dreaming about it. This place sticks with you.

I first dined here when I was a nineteen-year-old college student, and was instantly hooked. I've brought tons of actors, studio heads, artists, and food lovers over the years. It's always a huge hit.

I've pretty much followed the same routine since my first visit, which goes something like this (with very little variance):

I like to self-park so that I can admire the blue-lit trees on my walk in.

I admire the building's exterior and the name, Fonda San Miguel, carved in stone over the front door. Tom and Miguel went to great lengths to recreate the look and feel of the Mexican city San Miguel de Allende, which I've featured in my movies. They've perfectly captured its picturesque and jaw-dropping beauty.

I'm greeted by an always-delightful hostess. On my way to my seat, I pop over and say "hi" to Tom, who's usually drinking a glass of wine with friends. I pass Paco the Parrot in the birdcage.

I get to the table and order my favorite appetizers—tacos al pastor, tostadas compuestas, queso asado with chorizo verde, and tamales.

Miguel will inevitably circle the tables and say hello to guests.

I'll then order either the carne asada medium-rare (best in the world) with a duck enchilada on the side, or I'll get the puerco pibil. (This is where I first tasted that dish, and it was so good that it inspired me to have Johnny Depp's character in my film *Once Upon A Time In Mexico* literally kill for it.)

I'll then curl up with a margarita and down at least two bowls of the chipotle salsa as well as a few baskets of chips until the main dishes arrive.

I then finish off the dinner with either the tres leches or the immortal crepas de cajeta. My favorite part of the meal is watching new guests taste the crepas for the first time.

Okay, now I'm drooling as I'm writing this, and seriously craving some Fonda. I'd put down this computer right now and go get me some of that, but unfortunately it's after midnight and they're closed.

Fortunately for times like this, they have this handy cookbook, so now you can make a bit of their goodness at home.

I love to cook and have cracked open the first edition of this book so many times that I can vouch for its accuracy in capturing the spirit of these dishes.

It won't ever be exact, for everything in Miguel's restaurant kitchen is made with a level of love and artistry that is unmatched by any other establishment. There's definitely magic in that restaurant and they've squeezed that magic into this book. Try your hand at some of these recipes. It's very clever, actually; since I first got this book and tried making the dishes, I've ended up visiting Fonda San Miguel even MORE . . . not less. It's just so damn good.

There's that passion, again.

Robert Rodriguez
*Filmmaker, Musician, and*
*Founder of the El Rey Network*

When Miguel and I founded our first restaurant in Houston in 1972, we knew that we wanted to introduce the truly authentic and regional Mexican cuisines (with emphasis on the plural). To take on the ubiquitous and highly popular Tex-Mex was probably insane at the time, for the general public had never heard of "interior" or "classical" or "regional" Mexican food. There were no chipotle chiles, rarely even black beans (except maybe at a Cuban restaurant in Houston called Cardet's Cafe), and certainly no *huitlacoche* or anything in between. You had to be well traveled to the various regions of Mexico to have even an inkling of what we were attempting.

We had a grand dream, little experience, and a lot less cash when we began the unusual journey that we hope to capture in this Fonda San Miguel cookbook. One fortuitous event occurred in 1973 when Diana Kennedy walked into our little Houston restaurant. Diana had been told about two guys who were doing something similar to the traditional approaches that she had presented in her first book, *The Cuisines of Mexico*. Her response was something like, "You're on the right track, boys, and I'd like to help you"—to which we replied, as I recall, "We're already big fans of your book and would love that!" From that moment on, we were moving onward through the fog of toasting chiles, roasting tomatoes, and learning on the fly.

In the decades since, we've learned a great deal more about what we pioneered in Houston. In 1975 we moved to a much larger place in Austin, Fonda San Miguel. We are still learning. With the diversity of Mexico and its incredible culinary history, we could conceivably (but not easily) open twenty-five restaurants, each with a completely different menu.

The title of this book captures the dual focus of Fonda San Miguel—food and art. Our desire has always been to present intriguing Mexico at its best, and once the restaurant's cash flow improved, that desire led to the acquisition of art for the restaurant. It became an obsession! Today Fonda San Miguel displays the works of some of Mexico's best and most intriguing artists, past and present (and probably future). Distinctive Mexican art and decor is the best complement to authentic Mexican food!

Sometimes customers refer to the art displayed at Fonda San Miguel as a "collection." I guess that is what it's become, but putting together a coherent group of works was never my intention. In a rambling, almost haphazard way I have simply tried to find art for the restaurant. I never know when I'm going to find something interesting, and when I do, if it seems right and affordable, then I just buy it. Sometimes these impetuous purchases work, and sometimes they don't. As a consequence, we now have twice as much art in storage as we have on the walls. I've

*Opposite:*
*Chef Miguel Ravago and Tom Gilliland, founders of Fonda San Miguel*

15

come to learn the virtue of blank space: you can't cover every single inch with art. Oh, I suppose you can—I've done it myself—but the really great pieces look better when they have space around them. That's how we have tried to present our art. Even so, we do move the art around. Every now and then, all the paintings come down and get reframed, or put up in different locations. People will say, "Well, that's a new piece!" But it isn't—they're just noticing it for the first time.

In terms of a philosophy of collecting, I really don't have one. Valerie Piazza, the wife of a former director of the San Antonio Museum of Art, once said something to me that has become a kind of mantra: "When you look at something, does it sing to you?" That thought has stayed with me ever since. There are paintings that talk to me, but not all of them sing to me—so this criterion has saved us a lot of money. And over the years I've slowed down in buying art. Now I have to see something that sings a Puccini aria.

Sometimes I find things in unexpected places. One of my favorite pieces was being sold at an art show in a Mexico City park—for five or ten dollars.

It's rewarding to know that our customers enjoy the art. And it's also fascinating to observe their different reactions. Some people don't understand why on earth we decided to display a particular painting. And yet somebody else will walk up and say, "That's fabulous! Where did you get it?" I want people to be stimulated by what they see. I'm not a big fan of "safe" art, so I don't mind pushing the envelope.

The exciting journey of learning something that, in the restaurant business, is all about pleasing people has been remarkable. I love it as much today as the first day we opened in 1975. *The years go by quickly.*

—Tom Gilliland

 When I was growing up in Phoenix, there was a lot of cooking going on because it was such a big family. My mother and my sister and I lived with my grandparents, and my grandmother would cook three meals a day—not just for us but for her other grown children and their families, too. Sometimes there were as many as twenty people at the table, and twelve was a "slow" day! My grandmother was a wonderful cook because, for her, it was a hobby. She and my grandfather traveled around Mexico a lot, and she was always bringing back special ingredients from Veracruz and the other states. Although she was from the northern state of Sonora, seeing other parts of the country and sampling the different foods really fascinated her.

I was always curious about cooking, so my grandmother started showing me things like how to fill tamales. By the time I was six or seven, I was helping in the kitchen quite a bit. Then later on, when my mother and grandmother had to go somewhere, my sister and I would get to make dinner. The things we cooked didn't always turn out right, but the family was always very polite and ate it anyway. Gradually, I started cooking meals several times a week, especially when a large number of people were coming for dinner. My sister, who was four years older, would say, "You do it. You're better at it." She would then wash the dishes and clean up after me.

So even when I was pretty young, I think I knew I wanted to be a chef.

My first job when I moved to Houston was with Neiman-Marcus. Since I was bilingual, I helped entertain visitors from Mexico. I would take them to Mexican restaurants all over the city, but the food was never what they expected. In the restaurants at that time, there just wasn't any cooking like my grandmother's.

When Tom and I decided to open San Angel, our first restaurant, I had taken some cooking classes in Houston. But my formal training in authentic Mexican cuisine really began when I spent two weeks studying with Diana Kennedy in the kitchen of her New York apartment. She would send me off each morning with a grocery list, and then we would spend the rest of the day cooking the most wonderful dishes—which we gave to her neighbors and other people who lived in the building. Sometimes I showed her a few things I had learned from my grandmother, who was part Spanish, so her cooking had a bit of Spanish influence.

I've also learned a lot from studying and traveling with Patricia Quintana, who understands the French influence on Mexican cuisine. She is willing to experiment with ingredients that aren't strictly traditional. Patricia will say, "Well, we don't have that kind of chile right now, so let's use one that's fairly similar." Shirley King is someone else who gave me new skills; she came to Austin and taught me her secrets for working with seafood. Attending workshops with other chefs and learning from great instructors like María Dolores Torres Yzabal has given me skills and ideas that I constantly put to use at Fonda San Miguel.

After thirty years, cooking is still great fun for me. I especially enjoy the Hacienda Sunday Buffet, which always features four entrees from four different states in Mexico. This gives me a chance to help people learn about the food. If customers tell me they're planning a trip to a certain region of Mexico, I show them what dishes to taste so they'll know what kind of food to expect. Sometimes they come back and say the food wasn't as good as Fonda San Miguel's, and that's always nice to hear. I also enjoy training the kitchen staff and then standing back and seeing the good results. Working with the waiters is also interesting, teaching them how to show people the way to eat chile con queso and which type of tortilla goes best with certain dishes. I've always been curious about food, and I love to see people learn more about Mexican cuisine.

As Fonda San Miguel celebrates its fortieth anniversary, I want to thank our great customers who enjoy our food and keep coming back year after year. There are too many to name, but you know who you are. And I will never forget the special friends who have helped to make Fonda

San Miguel what it is today, such as Diana Kennedy, Patricia Quintana, Lucinda Hutson, Shirley King, and Bill Luft. Through it all, Tom Gilliland has been a wonderful business partner, trusting in my abilities and working to make our dream come true.

The restaurant's many loyal employees, from prep cooks to line cooks and servers, have been a big part of my life and helped me enormously as a chef all these years. Three of my assistants in the kitchen, Oscar Álvarez, Eusebio Álvarez, and Zenón Rentería, have worked by my side for many years, and I think they feel the passion in my cooking. They make sure the kitchen operates smoothly and efficiently so that we can keep our customers happy.

I will always be grateful for a family which, over the years, has given me unfailing support, a love of cooking, and a deep sense of pride in my great heritage—my dear mother Amelia Velásquez Galbraith, my grandmother Guadalupe Velásquez, my sister Betty Saenz, and my aunt Linda Mendivil. *¡Gracias por todo!*

And last but not least, many thanks to my partner, Philippe Mercier, for helping me gather all the recipes for this book and for taking such great care of me, always encouraging me to go forward and not look back.

—Chef Miguel Ravago

When I heard that Tom Gilliland and Miguel Ravago wanted to create a cookbook to commemorate the thirtieth anniversary of their popular restaurant Fonda San Miguel, I said a little prayer. I wanted to write the book more than I'd wanted anything in a very long time. I had been the restaurant's first pastry chef from 1977 to 1979, returned to work there in 1986–1987, and always had a strong sense of Fonda San Miguel's magical appeal. After my cooking career, I went on to become a journalist and eventually became the food editor at Austin's alternative newsweekly, the *Austin Chronicle*. I felt uniquely qualified to tell the Fonda San Miguel story, but I wasn't sure Tom and Miguel would see it that way. When Tom called me in December of 2002 and asked me to take charge of the project, I was thrilled! Work began in earnest in the fall of 2003, and Miguel and I spent many hours selecting and adapting the restaurant's recipes for the home cook. Writing the text has been an incredible learning experience, and I will always be grateful to Tom and Miguel for giving me this once-in-a-lifetime opportunity.

One of the genuine blessings involved in this project has been all the help and support I received from friends and fellow local culinary professionals. I want to express my heartfelt gratitude to the following people: my *Chronicle* employers, Louis Black and Nick Barbaro, for giving me the position that has made so many other things possible; Charles and Angela Smith for the new computer and all their other investments in my writing career; my sister Suzy for her encouragement; Suzann Dvorken for data entry support, commiseration, and unfailing willingness to be a good sounding board; Monica and Will Koenig for enthusiastically testing nearly a quarter of the recipes and always providing me with constructive comments; my *Chronicle* food writing colleagues Mary Margaret Pack, Wes Marshall, and Claudia Alarcón for their help with recipe testing; members of Austin's new chapter of Les Dames de Escoffier for their recipe-testing assistance—Pamela Nevarez, Michelle Haram, Jill Lewis, Karen Farnsworth, Joan Wood, Diane Tucker, Jane King, and Sahar Arafat-Ray; volunteer recipe testers Tricia Chandler, Cindy Haenel, Valerie Lesak, Amber O'Connor, and Morgan Hodgkins; my former *Chronicle* colleague Claiborne Smith for the historical article he wrote about Fonda San Miguel in 2002; and public relations consultant Forrest Preece for sharing the Fonda San Miguel newsletters he created over the past few years. I don't know how I could have made it without all of you.

During the last thirty years, the menu at Fonda San Miguel has been greatly enhanced by the inspiration and consultation of the legendary Diana Kennedy. As a result of her seminal cookbooks and frequent teaching excursions, Mrs. Kennedy is responsible for documenting and codifying hundreds of authentic interior Mexican dishes for an appreciative public. As a restaurant chef, Miguel Ravago adapted many of those recipes for presentation at Fonda San Miguel and for inclusion in this book. In addition to the family heirlooms from Miguel's mother and grandmother, the menu and the manuscript have also been enriched by recipes shared by Patricia Quintana, María Dolores Torres Yzabal, Shirley King, Susana Trilling, Philippe Mercier, Lucinda Hutson, and Roberto Santibáñez. I admire the work of each of them and appreciate their generosity.

I want to thank Kathy Shearer, Alison Tartt, Barbara Jezek, Tracey Maurer, and Julie Hettiger for turning my manuscript into a book that captures the beauty and magic I've always seen in Fonda San Miguel.

—Virginia B. Wood
2005

We are forever indebted to Virginia for her excellent work on the first edition, which has been ably continued, with the same dedication, by Cristina Potters.

—M.R. and T.G.

# The Fonda San Miguel Story

From 1845, when Texas joined the United States, to 1975, when Fonda San Miguel opened its doors to the residents of Austin, Texans yearned for food from Mexico's interior, regional Mexican food served on Texas turf. The dream came true: traditional and authentic Mexican dishes, prepared in the classic ways and available nearly every night, were finally here. From that time until now, Mexico has left its culinary mark not only on Texans, but also on all who have taken delight in relishing the true flavors of the Mexican table at Fonda San Miguel.

Tom Gilliland and Miguel Ravago continue to be the heart and soul of Fonda San Miguel. Tom, who spent a summer as a law student at the Universidad Nacional Autónoma de México in Mexico City, had learned to appreciate Mexico's regional dishes. As a child, Miguel was taught by his grandmother, Guadalupe Velásquez, to prepare many of those dishes in her kitchen. He convinced her to come to Houston in 1972 to help oversee the restaurant in its original incarnation, before it moved to Austin.

The Houston restaurant opened hot on the heels of the publication of one of the year's most popular cookbooks, Diana Kennedy's *The Cuisines of Mexico*. Tom and Miguel's copy was dog-eared and splattered when Mrs. Kennedy herself paid a surprise visit to the newly hatched restaurant. The three became good friends as she mentored the novice restaurant owners. With her initial help, the menus for Fonda San Miguel, which opened at its current location in 1975, took shape and took wing.

Customers were initially puzzled by a menu that held no hint of "Combination Plate #1" or platters of cheese enchiladas swimming in red sauce and topped with shredded lettuce, yellow cheese, and black olives. What was Mexican food, if not those? And where were the super-sized margaritas made from a mix? Diners instead were expected to choose their meals carefully, learning the then-exotic flavors of moles, mixiotes, and mangos and how best to combine them to make a complete and extremely satisfying dinner. Within a few years, however, Fonda San Miguel was the biggest hit in town, drawing hundreds of diners every night and praise to the heavens.

Tom and Miguel have talked about some of the trials and tribulations of bringing regional Mexican cooking from the interior to Texas, where Tex-Mex cooking rules. The challenges of sourcing ingredients in the mid-1970s were intense: where to find the items that are now available in our grocery stores—and particularly, where to find them in sufficient quantities for a 200-seat restaurant? The simplest and most necessary ingredients were an issue. For example, black beans had to be imported from Mexico in 55-gallon containers. When Tom and Miguel placed an order for specific chiles, destined for specific dishes, the wholesalers sent them a mixed bag of peppers that had to be carefully sorted before cooking could even begin. Fresh foods such as tomatillos were scarce, as were Mexican vanilla, Mexican chocolate, and Mexican cinnamon. Initially, all of those and more had to be imported. Precisely because of Fonda San Miguel's ongoing needs, Austin's wholesale grocers began to stock these once-exotic staples.

Due to Tom and Miguel's insistence on preserving the culinary traditions of regional, interior Mexico during the last forty years, very little Tex-Mex influence is seen in the restaurant. Regional cooking from the Mexican states of Oaxaca, Michoacán, Veracruz, Puebla, and Yucatan, as well as Mexico City, is the heart of the menu. Fonda San Miguel's interior Mexican focus has influenced not only Austin and its surrounding area, but also the rest of Texas and most places in the United States.

Why? Mexican food aficionados in the United States have become ever more knowledgeable about all things culinary as prepared south of the border. No longer content with only Tex-Mex (which is itself an important regional cuisine—of the southern United States; not Mexico), diners have begun to distinguish between foods from this Mexican state or that, and among the infinite varieties of chiles that make up Mexico's range of *picante* (spicy heat), and have discovered the subtle differences among high-end sipping tequilas and, more recently, among the *mezcales* from several states in Mexico.

Miguel's role in the restaurant is executive chef. His decisions in the kitchen affect your experience at the table; his constant testing and tasting as new preparations come into existence make it certain that you and your family and friends will delight in whichever dishes you choose from the menu. Tom has been in charge of hiring and supervising the front of the house, handling remodeling and décor, acquiring breathtaking art for each room at Fonda San Miguel, and doing most everything else except running the kitchen. Their personalities genuinely complement one another and make the restaurant what it is: personal and beautiful, with a guaranteed-to-be-exquisite meal whenever you choose to dine. For the past four decades, with just a brief hiatus to reconfigure and redefine their business partnership, these two gentlemen—and gentlemen they truly are—have brought to Austin and to the world the best of Mexico's regional cuisines.

Long ago, when I was just beginning to learn about Mexican food, the name Fonda San Miguel kept coming up in conversation, in restaurant reviews, and in other reading addressed to food professionals. My honest thoughts at that time: *What could a couple of Texans possibly know about the real food of Mexico? Texas is all about Tex-Mex!* Later, I heard that two of my favorite Mexican chefs were working in the Fonda San Miguel kitchen. First Ricardo Muñoz Zurita, and later

Roberto Santibáñez, both extraordinary chefs from Mexico City, turned up in the reviews I was reading about the restaurant. Both are men I respect; both are longtime friends and colleagues. I kept asking myself, *What are those talented guys doing at a Mexican restaurant in Texas?*

It took me a long time to learn what was really happening at Fonda San Miguel, and I've come to call my early eye-rolling by its true name: contempt prior to investigation. Once I came to Austin, went to the restaurant, and met that "couple of *Texans*," I was a convert to the Fonda San Miguel way of cooking, way of hosting, and way of constant striving even in the face of many overwhelmingly successful decades in business. No one, from the cleaning staff to the owners themselves, rests on his or her laurels.

Even in Mexico it would be hard to find a restaurant as beautiful as Fonda San Miguel. It is carefully and generously filled with the best of Mexico's popular crafts and fine paintings by its most distinguished artists. From the entryway to the restrooms, from floor to ceiling, there is beauty everywhere one looks. Attention to detail, so important and often so overlooked, constantly amazes. Each light fixture, each perfectly set tile, the recently carved and colored bar front, each table and every chair, each plate and every soup spoon, give testimony to Tom and Miguel's desire to offer their generations of clients the absolute best of everything.

From the button-popping excesses of the Hacienda Sunday Brunch Buffet, to a birthday celebration with family and friends, to the coziness of stopping in for an evening drink—tequila straight up with a sangrita back? Maybe a guava margarita?—there is the warm sensation of coming home. There's always conversation, always recognition, always inclusion. Small wonder the crowds keep coming to Fonda San Miguel: it's a Mexican home away from home.

Not many restaurants flourish for a year, let alone for decades. Celebrated in Texas, renowned in the rest of the United States, and much respected in Mexico, Fonda San Miguel contin-

Art by Pedro Friedeberg, 1983–1990 menu

Dining room, late 1970s

LA COMIDA DE MEXICO

FONDA SAN MIGUEL

ues not only to flourish, but to improve. This edition of its story includes new recipes, a section devoted to fine tequilas and *mezcales*, and numerous fresh photographs that show off new paintings and beautiful new menu items that will make your mouth water. With such spirit, I believe this enchanting Austin institution will go on for another forty years.

—Cristina Potters, 2016

*Menu art, 1975*

# TEQUILA Y MEZCAL

Which Is Which and Why

Tequila is an alcoholic beverage made everywhere in Mexico from any old cactus and drunk till you're—well, till you're drunk, right? That's how it was when you were newly twenty-one and legal, having a spring break moment or two on a south-of-the-border beach, and pounding back shots till . . . well, you might remember.

And mezcal? That's another Mexican alcoholic beverage made from ground-up cactus by Mexican laborers who make their own moonshine. Yes?

Not exactly. Mexican production of these two liquors has changed remarkably in recent decades.

For starters, tequila was awarded its Denominación de Origen as long ago as 1978. The D.O. regulates what is and what is not tequila, and where tequila can and cannot be produced. Tequila, primarily a commercial product, may only be made in small sections of the five Mexican states where the Weber blue agave is permitted to grow: Guanajuato, Jalisco, Michoacán, Nayarit, and Tamaulipas. By further regulation, tequila must be labeled as to whether it is made from 100 percent Weber blue agave or whether it is mixto—part blue agave, part water and sugar added during distillation. Be careful to read the label indicating contents, and whenever possible, buy and drink 100 percent Weber blue agave tequila.

Here are the Denominación de Origen rules that define the type of tequila in any bottle:

Blanco (also known as silver, or white): clear tequila aged no more than sixty days in stainless steel drums, if aged at all. Often tastes strongly of raw agave. Use these for margaritas, palomas, and other mixed drinks

Joven (young) or oro (gold): young tequilas that were primarily responsible for those drunken days of yesteryear. They can be flavored and colored with caramel or oak extract or other additives and, consumed in quantity, are sure to cause a serious hangover. Steer clear.

Reposado: aged or "rested" in oak casks for three months to a year. The casks give a soft oak flavor to the agave; reposado is arguably the most popular type of tequila.

Añejo: "old" tequila aged in oak barrels for a minimum of one year; the best is aged between eighteen months and three years, which produces a darker, golden color, a mild, earthy flavor, and a very smooth mouth feel. Drink it straight.

Extra-Añejo: a premium long-aged tequila made to be sipped straight and slow, like fine old single-malt scotch whiskey.

Mezcal, on the other hand, is made from a number of different maguey cacti, depending on which producers make it. The most commonly used cactus is the Espadín maguey, but others are Tobalá and Cupreata. Mezcal is a much less commercialized product than tequila and is often made in small batches, just a few times a year, to be sold in very limited quantities by private vendors. Mezcal is produced in Mexico wherever maguey cacti grow, although the states with the highest production are Durango, Guanajuato, Guerrero, Michoacán, Oaxaca, San Luis Potosí, Tamaulipas, and Zacatecas.

Mezcal sometimes has quite a smoky flavor. Legend has it that smoky mezcal was first created after a mezcalero (producer) accidentally burned a batch of cactus and went ahead with his production anyway. When it's not smoky, mezcal often has hints of pine forest and wildflower.

Both types are enjoyed either straight or with mixers. If taken straight, mezcal is customarily served with a small plate of fresh orange slices eaten as a chaser as you sip your drink. Be sure to sprinkle the orange slices with sal de gusano—a spicy-tangy mix of sea salt, dried red chile de árbol, and toasted red maguey worms. Don't knock it till you've tried it—sal de gusano is absolutely delicious.

Mezcal is enjoying a huge boom in popularity. If you haven't already, try a sipping glass of mezcal with us at Fonda San Miguel.

# TEQUILA SHOTS— STRAIGHT UP!

*2 ounces silver tequila*

*2 ounces prepared sangrita*

Serve each side by side in a separate *caballito*—a shot glass.

# SPICY RED SNAPPER BLOODY MARY— OR MARÍA!

This is your spicy Bloody Mary but with a fun twist. You can make it with your choice of gin, vodka, tequila, or mezcal.

*5 ice cubes*

*1 6-ounce can tomato juice (the best you can get)*

*2 ounces gin, vodka, tequila, or mezcal*

*2 tablespoons freshly squeezed lemon juice*

*2 tablespoons bottled hot pepper sauce (Salsa Valentina)*

*2 tablespoons Worcestershire sauce*

*½ teaspoon brine from a jar of olives*

*1 pinch hot chili powder*

*1 pinch garlic powder*

*1 pinch ground cumin*

*¼ teaspoon celery salt*

*¼ teaspoon freshly ground pepper*

*¼ teaspoon prepared or freshly grated horseradish*

### Garnish

*1 celery stalk with leaves (from the heart of the celery)*

*1 small dill pickle*

*2 stuffed green olives*

*1 freshly cut lemon wedge*

Place ice cubes in a cocktail shaker. Pour in all liquid ingredients and season with all the rest. Cover and shake until the outside of the shaker is frosty.

Pour all contents, including ice, into a 12-ounce highball glass. Before serving, garnish with celery, pickle, olive, and lemon wedge. Serves 1.

# SANGRITA A LA LUCINDA

Lucinda Hutson, author of *¡Viva Tequila!* and a dear friend of Fonda San Miguel, makes the best sangrita we have ever tasted. She has graciously allowed us to pass her recipe on to you.

*4 cups freshly squeezed orange juice*

*1½ cups 100 percent natural pomegranate juice*

*½ cup freshly squeezed lime juice (preferably from small, round Mexican limes)*

*8 to 12 ounces commercially bottled salsa (Salsa Valentina or Salsa Tamazula)*

*Salt to taste*

Mix ingredients together and chill overnight or longer—it just gets better with age. Adjust the flavorings *al gusto* (to your taste) for the perfect balance. Serve chilled in *caballitos* (shot glasses) to accompany shots of tequila.

Sangrita will keep for more than a week if refrigerated. Makes approximately 7 cups (24 shots).

# PAPER HEART TEQUILA MARTINI

The key to a great martini is to make certain it's served ice cold.

*1¾ ounces Don Julio tequila reposado*

*1 ounce freshly squeezed orange juice*

*½ ounce cold ginger tea*

*¼ ounce freshly squeezed lime juice (preferably from small, round Mexican limes)*

*⅓ ounce maple syrup*

*2 slices fresh ginger, each the size of your thumbnail*

Shake all ingredients with ice and strain into a chilled martini glass. Serves 1.

# TEQUILA OR MEZCAL COCKTAILS

Each of these delightfully refreshing cocktails bears the name of a very special member of the Fonda San Miguel family. We're happy to honor them and you'll be thrilled with the drinks!

## Señor Bogart

*2 ounces tequila or mezcal*

*¼ ounce Cointreau*

*Juice of ½ lime (preferably from small, round Mexican limes)*

*1 teaspoon simple syrup*

*1 chunk fresh pineapple*

Shake with crushed ice and strain into a highball glass with sugared rim. Serves 1.

## La Dita

*½ ounce tequila reposado or mezcal*

*¾ ounce crème de cassis*

*½ ounce freshly squeezed lime juice (preferably from small, round Mexican limes)*

*Ginger ale or ginger beer*

*Wedge of lime (preferably a small, round Mexican lime)*

Fill a Collins glass with ice. Add the tequila (or mezcal) and the cassis. Top off with ginger ale or ginger beer. Add lime wedge. Serves 1.

## Don Paco Hibiscus Margarita

*1 ounce mezcal*

*1 ounce hibiscus syrup*

*½ ounce freshly squeezed lime juice (preferably from small, round Mexican limes)*

Shake over ice. Serve straight up in a martini glass. Serves 1.

## Hibiscus Syrup

*1 cup water*

*½ cup dried hibiscus flowers*

*¾ cup sugar*

Bring water to boil, add hibiscus and sugar, and cook over medium to high heat for another 10 minutes. Remove from stove, let cool, pour through a strainer, then store in a refrigerator. The syrup lasts for up to 10 days.

*Hand carved by Jesus "Chucho" Moreno from Mexico City, who has designed and painted the interior and exterior of Fonda San Miguel for many years.*

# ANTOJITOS Y BEBIDAS
## Appetizers & Beverages

Every aspect of the original Fonda San Miguel menu, based on the unfamiliar cuisine from Mexico's interior, involved some education of the Austin dining public. Nowhere was the learning curve any steeper than with appetizers, the site of a mighty skirmish. Tex-Mex restaurant tradition dictates that meals begin with baskets of fresh tostada chips and little bowls of hot sauce. When the restaurant's original menu consultant, Diana Kennedy, pointed out that this practice was inconsistent with traditional Mexican cuisine, Tom and Miguel decided to stand pat against the Tex-Mex influence. The Austin dining public proved to be stubborn, however. After a contest of wills, Tom and Miguel saw the wisdom of offering chips and hot sauce to their customers. But San Miguel's assortment of Mexican regional appetizers is tempting enough in itself to keep most people from filling up on chips.

When Fonda San Miguel opened in 1975, the Texas tradition of consuming frozen margarita cocktails with Mexican food was only a few years old. Remarkably, liquor by the drink had only been legal in post-Prohibition Texas since 1971. Tom and Miguel were determined that the bar would be an attraction in itself, an oasis where customers could relax on the leafy patio, enjoy a cocktail or an agua fresca, and convince themselves that they had slipped away to Mexico. Extensive research went into the development of the first fresh lime margarita recipe, and Fonda San Miguel's margaritas remain some of the most popular in Austin today. Cocktail trends come and go, but the bar at San Miguel is well known for its reliable take on south-of-the-border libations. Mix up a refreshing Paloma or a unique Silver Coin Margarita (made with watermelon-infused silver tequila), and you'll see why.

José María de Servín

*¡Emborráchate!* ca. 1965. Oil on tissue paper, 28 × 18½ inches.

José María de Servín

*¡No te emborraches!* ca. 1965. Oil on tissue paper, 28 × 18½ inches.

There's an interesting story behind the two companion paintings that hang in the bar—a permanent location because of their titles (which mean "Get Drunk!" and "Don't Get Drunk!" in English). They were painted sometime in the mid-sixties. A good friend of the painter's ran a Mexican arts and crafts store in Monterrey, which, at the time, was the best in all of Mexico. Prior to that, the gentleman had operated Hotel Carapan in Monterrey. Many years ago, when Miguel and I were looking for decorative pieces for the restaurant, we decided to visit this gentleman because of his reputation for having excellent taste in Mexican arts and crafts. We were finally shown these two paintings, which were among the owner's favorite possessions. They were hidden away in a storeroom, covered with inches of dust. The man agreed to sell them after we promised that he would get a chance to buy them back if we ever decided to part with them.

Then he told us the story of how the artist came to paint them. One evening, when he and the artist were drinking together in the bar of his hotel, he said to his friend, "You know, I don't have anything of yours to hang here in the bar." The artist said, "All right, bring me some paper." "Now?" the man asked. "Yes, now." So while they sat there, the artist painted these two pieces. But the only paper to be found was tissue paper. Consequently, these two paintings are very delicate.

Some years ago an elderly couple came to Fonda San Miguel for dinner and, after noticing the paintings, asked where they had come from. When I told them the story, tears came to the woman's eyes. She and her husband had stayed in the old hotel before it was torn down and knew the owner. Seeing the paintings again after so many years brought back memories.

T.G.

# SALSA ROJA
## Red Table Sauce

Mexican restaurants in Texas take great pride in their table sauces, traditionally served as a complimentary appetizer before the meal with baskets of warm tostada chips. Although Tom and Miguel initially resisted, their clientele convinced them that serving chips and salsa was the one Tex-Mex convention they would have to adopt for customer satisfaction. This red table sauce is equally good fresh and warm from the stove or chilled from the refrigerator.

*4 large tomatoes, roasted and peeled* ✿

*Half of a medium white onion, chopped*

*2 to 4 serrano chiles, roasted and chopped* ✿

*1 garlic clove, chopped*

*1 tablespoon vegetable oil*

*Sea salt to taste*

Combine the tomatoes, onion, chiles, and garlic in a *molcajete* or food processor and blend to a chunky puree. In a heavy, 12-inch skillet over medium heat, heat the oil. Add the tomato mixture, reduce heat to low, and cook for about 5 minutes. Add salt to taste. Serve warm or chill in the refrigerator for later use. Makes 3 cups.

# SALSA VERDE
## Green Table Sauce

Dinner at Fonda San Miguel begins with bowls of red and green signature salsas and baskets of warm tostada chips. The crisp, slightly salty chips arrive fresh daily from the locally owned El Milagro Tortilla Factory. They are every bit as addictive as this tangy green salsa.

*12 tomatillos, husked* ✿

*2 to 4 serrano chiles, chopped* ✿

*10 sprigs cilantro, chopped*

*2 garlic cloves, chopped*

*½ cup chopped white onion*

*2 tablespoons vegetable oil*

*1 teaspoon sea salt*

*Sugar to taste*

Put the tomatillos in a 3-quart nonreactive saucepan and cover with water. Cook over medium heat until the tomatillos soften and their green color begins to fade, about 8 to 10 minutes. Drain the tomatillos, reserving 1 cup of the cooking liquid. Combine the cooked tomatillos, chiles, cilantro, garlic, and onion in a blender and blend, using up to 1 cup of the reserved cooking liquid to make a smooth, liquid puree. Heat the oil in the same saucepan over medium heat. Add the puree and salt; cook for 8 to 10 minutes, stirring often. Check seasoning and add a little sugar if tomatillos are bitter. Serve warm or chilled. Makes 3½ to 4 cups.

## Variation

Cool the sauce and puree it in a blender with the flesh of 1 ripe avocado and ½ cup sour cream. Use as a dip or a topping for chicken-filled Enchiladas San Miguel.

# GORDITAS WITH TINGA POBLANA

*Tinga poblana*, a mixture of shredded pork and delicious seasonings, is one of the signature dishes of the city of Puebla, Mexico. Stuffed into *gorditas* (little fatties), it's a terrific addition to a brunch, midday meal, or supper.

### Shredded Pork and Chorizo Filling

*2 pounds fresh pork shoulder*

*1 whole white onion, quartered*

*2 pounds fresh, ripe red tomatoes*

*½ pound fresh chorizo, casings removed*

*4 cloves garlic, chopped*

*2 whole white onions, chopped*

*¼ cup flat-leaf parsley, chopped*

*4 whole canned chipotle chiles in adobo, chopped*

*4 tablespoons adobo sauce from the chiles*

*Salt and pepper to taste*

Bring 3 quarts of water to a boil. Add the pork and the quartered white onion, reduce to a simmer, and cook for 1 hour. Remove the meat from the liquid and cool. When the pork is cool enough to handle, shred the meat using two forks, scraping with the grain. Cover and reserve.

Roast the tomatoes on a griddle over high flame. When the tomato skins are blistered and split, seal them in a plastic bag to "sweat" for a few minutes to loosen the skins. Peel, core, and chop the tomatoes.

Sauté the chorizo for 5 minutes together with the chopped garlic, onions, and parsley. Then add the shredded pork, the tomatoes, the chipotle chiles, and the adobo sauce. Simmer for another 10 minutes, uncovered. Add salt and pepper to taste.

### Masa (Dough) for Gorditas

*2 tablespoons freshly rendered pork lard or vegetable shortening*

*1 pound fresh corn masa*

*½ teaspoon salt*

*¼ cup flour*

*1 teaspoon baking powder*

*Vegetable oil, refried beans, shredded lettuce, crumbled white Mexican cheese*

Using a mixer, whip the shortening until fluffy. Add the masa, salt, flour, and baking powder. Mix together and allow the masa to rest for about 5 minutes before making the *gorditas*.

### "Bake and Fry" Method

Preheat oven to 400 degrees. Divide the masa into 12 pieces. Pat each piece into a circle about 3 to 3½ inches in diameter and ¼-inch thick. Place the disks on a baking sheet and bake until they are crusty. Meanwhile, heat about ½ inch of vegetable oil in a frying pan. Taking care not to burn yourself, place the *gorditas* in the oil, and watch out for splatter. The *gorditas* will puff up. Remove when golden brown and drain on paper towels. Slit each *gordita* open and stuff with refried beans, *tinga poblana*, shredded lettuce, and salsa, and top with crumbled cheese. Serves 12.

# CEVICHE VERACRUZANO ✽

## Ceviche, Veracruz Style

Tom and Miguel discovered this recipe for ceviche at a restaurant in Boca del Rio in the coastal state of Veracruz. A simple recipe that appears on both the appetizer and dinner menu as well as on the Hacienda Sunday Brunch Buffet, it is a guaranteed hit at parties. It keeps well, up to two days, and should be served with tostada chips and ice-cold beer. If black drum or redfish isn't available, you can use red snapper, tilapia, or trout.

*1 pound skinned black drum or redfish fillets, cut into ½-inch cubes*

*Juice of 8 large limes (about ½ cup)*

*4 to 5 pickled jalapeños, drained (or fewer for a milder dish) ✽*

*2 medium tomatoes, seeded and chopped*

*¼ cup olive oil*

*½ teaspoon dried Mexican oregano*

*½ teaspoon sea salt*

*½ teaspoon ground black pepper*

*Leaf lettuce for lining dish*

*Avocado slices*

*Lime wedges*

Place fish cubes in a nonreactive bowl and pour lime juice over them; toss to coat well. Cover the bowl with plastic wrap and refrigerate for at least 5 hours or overnight. Stir occasionally with a wooden spoon. Chop jalapeños and add them to the fish, along with tomatoes, oil, and seasonings. Toss well and drain. Serve chilled in a bowl or footed glass lined with lettuce leaves and garnished with avocado slices and lime wedges. Serves 6.

# VUELVE A LA VIDA

## Return to Life

Miguel learned this recipe from our dear friend Nushie Chancellor, who worked for us at Fonda San Miguel. It's THE best recipe for this seafood cocktail.

*4 ounces precooked chunky crab claw meat*

*4 ounces uncooked bay scallops*

*4 ounces precooked small squid, cut into ¼-inch rings*

*4 ounces uncooked skinless fish: black drum, redfish, or any other firm fish, cut into ½-inch cubes*

*¼ cup freshly squeezed lime juice (preferably from small, round Mexican limes)*

*4 ounces cooked shrimp*

*1 cup ketchup*

*1½ teaspoons Worcestershire sauce*

*1 large orange, juiced*

*1 tablespoon red wine vinegar*

*1 teaspoon dried Mexican oregano*

*2 tablespoons olive oil*

*½ white onion, chopped*

*1 large tomato, chopped*

*½ cup cilantro leaves, chopped*

*1 chipotle chile en adobo, chopped*

*1 jalapeño en escabeche (pickled), chopped*

*1 cup canned small peas*

*½ cup stuffed green olives, sliced*

*Salt and freshly ground black pepper to taste*

*Lime wedges*

Place the crab meat, scallops, squid, fish, and lime juice in a glass bowl to marinate 3 to 4 hours in the refrigerator, making sure to mix occasionally and be certain that the seafood gets "cooked" in the lime juice. Do not add shrimp until ready to serve.

After marinating, drain and add the ketchup, Worcestershire sauce, orange juice, vinegar, Mexican oregano, and oil. Next, add the lime juice drained from the marinating seafood. Add onion, tomato, cilantro, chipotle, jalapeño chiles, peas, and olives. Taste and correct the salt and pepper.

Serve in cocktail glasses, each placed on a small dish surrounded with *totopos* (corn tortilla chips). Garnish with lime wedges. Serves 4.

# TOSTADAS DE COCHINITA PIBIL

## Tostadas with Pit-Cooked Pork

One of Fonda San Miguel's most popular appetizers, these tostadas are topped with shredded pork that has been seasoned and slow-cooked in the classic *pibil* style of the Yucatan Peninsula.

*6 or 7 large corn tortillas*
*Cochinita Pibil (see separate recipe)*
*Cebollas Rojas en Escabeche (see separate recipe) for garnish*
*Leaf lettuce, chopped, for garnish*
*Shredded radishes for garnish*

Preheat oven to 250 degrees. Using a 2½-inch round cookie cutter, cut cocktail-size rounds out of the tortillas, about 4 or 5 rounds per tortilla. Spray a baking sheet with nonstick cooking spray and place the rounds on the baking sheet. Bake in preheated oven until crisp and golden, about 45 minutes. Set aside.

Prepare Cochinita Pibil. Shred the cooked meat with the fingers or two forks. Spoon the meat onto the baked tostadas and garnish with Cebollas Rojas en Escabeche, chopped leaf lettuce, and shredded radishes. Serves 8 (3 or 4 tostadas per person).

# CALAMARES
## Fried Squid

The New York chef, teacher, and cookbook author Shirley King is one of Miguel's dearest friends and a longtime friend and supporter of the restaurant. She was generous enough to share this excellent recipe for calamari, which originally appeared in her cookbook *Fish—The Basics*, published in 1998. She often combines squid and crawfish tails when making this dish. Shirley's secret to perfectly crisp calamari is a good deep-frying thermometer and good technique—she allows the frying oil to return to a temperature of 375 degrees between each batch. This appetizer is good with Chipotle Mayonnaise as well as your favorite salsa, tartar sauce, or remoulade sauce.

*1 quart vegetable oil, or enough so that oil is 2 inches deep in a Dutch oven or deep fryer*

*6 to 8 ounces squid, cleaned and cut into ¼-inch rings*

*½ cup all-purpose flour, seasoned with 1 teaspoon sea salt, ½ teaspoon ground black pepper, and ½ teaspoon cayenne pepper (or to taste)*

*2 lemon wedges*

*2 sprigs parsley*

## Chipotle Mayonnaise

Makes 1¼ cups.

*1 cup Hellmann's mayonnaise*

*2 chipotle chiles in adobo sauce* ✽

*1 garlic clove, minced*

*Zest and juice of 1 lime*

*Sea salt and ground black pepper to taste*

Prepare the Chipotle Mayonnaise. Combine all ingredients in a blender and pulse until smooth. Refrigerate until ready to serve.

　　To prepare the calamari, heat oil to 375 degrees in a heavy Dutch oven or deep fryer. Toss a few of the squid rings in the seasoned flour and coat well; shake off the excess using a small sieve or strainer. Drop the pieces of squid into the oil; do not allow them to touch. Fry 10 to 15 seconds (don't overcook) and remove the fried pieces of squid using a slotted spoon. Drain on paper towels and keep in a warm oven while you fry the remaining batches. Make sure the oil returns to 375 degrees before adding each batch. Serve hot with lemon wedges, parsley sprigs, and Chipotle Mayonnaise.

# HIGADITOS CON HIGOS Y JALAPEÑOS
## Chicken Livers with Figs and Jalapeños

This may sound like a strange combination, but the sweet/sour/spicy joining of figs, onions, jalapeño, and vinegar is a perfect foil for the livers and their savory richness. These are great served with cocktails.

*5 tablespoons unsalted butter*

*2 red onions, peeled and thinly sliced*

*1 fresh jalapeño pepper, chopped*

*1²/₃ cups chicken livers, trimmed of sinew*

*3 tablespoons granulated sugar*

*4 ripe figs, stems removed and halved*

*5 tablespoons red wine vinegar*

*4 slices sourdough bread, toasted*

*Extra virgin olive oil*

*¼ cup flat leaf parsley, roughly chopped*

*Zest of ½ lemon*

Melt half the butter in a large frying pan. Add the onions, jalapeño, and a pinch of salt. Cook over gentle heat for 20 minutes, until the onion is soft and starting to brown. Remove to a plate and set aside.

Thoroughly pat dry the chicken livers on paper towels. Season well with salt and pepper. Add the remaining butter to the frying pan and, once it foams, add the livers. Fry over medium heat for about 2 minutes on each side or until cooked through. Cook in batches if needed. Set aside with the onions.

Turn the heat to medium-low. Sprinkle the sugar over the pan and add the figs, cut side down. Cook for about 1 minute, until the cut side starts to bubble and brown; turn over. Add the vinegar and bubble for a few seconds, until syrupy. Return the onions and livers to the pan. Correct the seasonings and stir together.

Spoon the fig and liver mixture over the toast. Splash with olive oil and sprinkle with parsley and lemon zest before serving. Serves 4.

# PANUCHOS
## Fried Filled Tortillas

These Yucatecan panuchos are wonderful to serve with cocktails to a few guests at home. They are very easy to make and also work well as part of a buffet table.

### Tortillas

> *2 cups masa harina*
>
> *3 tablespoons all-purpose flour*
>
> *1¼ cups warm water*
>
> *1 cup warm Frijoles Negros (see separate recipe)*
>
> *Vegetable oil for frying*

### Toppings

> *2 cups Cochinita Pibil (see separate recipe)*
>
> *Cebollas Rojas en Escabeche (see separate recipe)*
>
> *Sliced avocados*
>
> *Chopped fresh cilantro*
>
> *Grated queso fresco or Monterey Jack cheese*

Combine the masa harina and the flour. Slowly add the water, mix well, and knead. Divide the dough into 12 balls and press into small tortillas. Cook the tortillas on a hot griddle, turning each one. They should puff up as they cook, but if they don't, press lightly on the tortilla to induce it to inflate. Remove the tortillas from the griddle and cool slightly. Make a pocket in each tortilla by making an incision in the part that puffed up, about ¼ inch from the edge.

Place 1 tablespoon of the beans in each tortilla pocket and flatten the opening to seal. Cover with a damp cloth.

Pour oil into a frying pan to the depth of ½ inch. Heat to 350 degrees. Fry the panuchos until they are crisp around the edges. Drain on paper towels.

Plate the panuchos and top with the shredded Cochinita Pibil, onions, avocado slices, cilantro, and cheese.

Serve with the salsa of your choice. Serves 4 to 6 as an appetizer or 3 as a main dish.

# FONDA SAN MIGUEL CHICKEN LIVER PATÉ

Around the turn of the twentieth century, all things French became high fashion in Mexico. Patés were popular then and are still much appreciated today.

*13 ounces chicken livers, trimmed*

*10 ounces butter (2½ sticks), diced*

*1 clove garlic, minced*

*3 shallots or ½ white onion, minced*

*½ teaspoon fresh thyme leaves, chopped*

*1 or 2 fresh serrano chiles, minced (optional)*

*2 tablespoons brandy*

*½ teaspoon nutmeg, freshly grated*

*Salt and black pepper to taste*

*2 ounces butter (4 tablespoons), melted for topping*

Trim the chicken livers, then rinse and pat them dry with paper towels.

In a large frying pan, melt 1 ounce of butter over medium heat. Add the garlic, shallots, thyme, and serrano chiles; cook, stirring, for 5 minutes until they are softened.

Add the livers and cook until they are brown on the outside but pink on the inside. Pour in the brandy and cook for an additional 10 seconds. Add the remaining butter and nutmeg to the pan.

Set aside until the butter softens, then purée the mixture in a blender or food processor until smooth. Do this in batches if necessary. Correct the salt and pepper.

Pour the mixture into a 24-ounce terrine dish and chill. Melt the remaining butter and pour it over the paté. Cover with plastic wrap and refrigerate at least 3 to 4 hours prior to serving. Remove paté from the refrigerator approximately 15 minutes before serving. Serve with crusty bread or *totopos* (corn chips).

Serves 12.

# QUESADILLAS DE HONGOS
## Mushroom Quesadillas

The basis of any quesadilla, as its name implies, is *queso*—preferably a mild white cheese that melts easily. But beyond this ingredient, almost anything can go into the filling—from vegetables to beans to leftover meats. The versatility of the quesadilla is almost unlimited.

*2 tablespoons safflower oil*

*1 medium white onion, chopped*

*2 garlic cloves, minced*

*3 serrano chiles, minced*

*1 1-pound package mushrooms, cleaned and thinly sliced*

*2 tablespoons chopped epazote leaves (optional)* ✽

*Sea salt to taste*

*12 corn or flour tortillas*

*2 cups (8 ounces) shredded Monterey Jack cheese*

*Salsa de Chile Chipotle*

Heat oil in a heavy sauté pan over medium heat. Add onion, garlic, and chiles and cook until wilted and transparent, but not browned, about 2 minutes. Add mushrooms and epazote, reduce heat to low, and cook an additional 15 to 20 minutes, stirring often, or until juices are absorbed. Add salt to taste. Spoon the mushroom mixture onto each tortilla; divide the cheese and sprinkle evenly over the filling. Fold the tortillas in half. Heat a lightly greased comal or griddle over medium heat. Using a wide, flat spatula, gently slide a filled tortilla onto the hot comal. Use the spatula to lightly press the halves of the tortilla together while the quesadilla is cooking on the bottom. Cook 2 to 3 minutes, or until bottom becomes golden brown around the edges and the cheese is melted. Carefully flip the quesadilla over and cook for an additional 1 to 2 minutes, or until the bottom is golden. Remove to a serving platter and repeat with the remaining quesadillas. Serve hot with fresh Salsa de Chile Chipotle. Serves 4 to 6 as an appetizer.

## Salsa de Chile Chipotle
Makes 2 cups.

*5 or 6 chipotle chiles in adobo sauce*

*4 garlic cloves, roasted*

*10 Roma tomatoes (about 2 pounds), roasted until blistered*

*1 tablespoon peanut oil*

*Sea salt to taste*

*Water as needed*

Combine chiles, roasted garlic, and roasted, unpeeled tomatoes in a blender; blend until smooth.

## Variations

For Quesadillas de Pollo, substitute the Chicken Filling for Enchiladas San Miguel instead of the mushroom filling. Assemble the quesadillas as directed.

For Quesadillas de Chile Poblano, substitute Rajas Cebollas instead of the mushroom filling. Assemble the quesadillas as directed.

# ESQUITES MEXICO CITY STYLE

*Esquites* (mildly spicy and flavorful corn kernels), sold by the cupful by street vendors all over Mexico City, make a terrific appetizer with drinks before dinner. For a creative touch, serve them in shot glasses with tiny ice cream spoons.

> *2 tablespoons freshly rendered pork lard or butter*
>
> *¼ white onion, finely diced*
>
> *3 or 4 dried whole chiles de árbol*
>
> *4 cups fresh corn kernels (not frozen or canned)*
>
> *Several sprigs of fresh epazote leaves, chopped (optional but desirable)*
>
> *Sea salt to taste*

In a large frying pan, melt the lard or butter. Add the diced onion, whole chiles, and corn kernels. Stirring frequently, cook over medium heat until the onion is translucent. Add the chopped epazote and a pinch of salt. Continue to cook over low heat for about 5 minutes more. Taste and correct the salt. Serves 8 to 10 as an appetizer, or 4 as a side dish for lunch or dinner.

# CHILE CON QUESO ✿
## Sautéed Chiles with Cheese

When Fonda San Miguel opened in 1975, Tex-Mex lovers were surprised and confused by this Chihuahua-style Chile con Queso. They were accustomed to chiles and tomatoes in a thin, American cheese–style sauce served as a dip with tostada chips. This version from one of the northern states of Mexico is thick with savory sautéed vegetables and is best when wrapped in warm homemade flour or corn tortillas like a taco. This same recipe is used as the filling for the San Miguel Omelet.

> *6 tablespoons vegetable oil*
>
> *1 medium white onion, sliced thin*
>
> *1 to 2 poblano chiles, roasted, peeled, seeded, and cut into ¼-inch strips* ✿
>
> *1 medium tomato, peeled and thinly sliced*
>
> *1 scant cup milk*
>
> *2 cups (8 ounces) shredded Monterey Jack or Muenster cheese*
>
> *1½ teaspoons sea salt*
>
> *Fresh flour or corn tortillas, warmed*

In a heavy saucepan, heat oil over medium heat. Add onion slices and cook until they are wilted and transparent but not browned. Add chiles and tomato; cook for 8 to 10 minutes. Add milk and cook over low heat for an additional 3 minutes. Add the cheese and salt and stir until the cheese melts. (Or put the hot vegetable and milk mixture in a bowl, top with the shredded cheese, and heat about 2 minutes in the microwave, stirring once or twice.) Transfer to a serving bowl and serve hot with fresh tortillas. Serves 6.

# CROQUETAS DE CAMARÓN

## Shrimp Croquettes

These make a perfect little explosion of flavor in your mouth, and are a great party dish.

*3 tablespoons olive oil*

*1 teaspoon finely chopped onion*

*1 teaspoon finely chopped serrano chile*

*¼ cup all-purpose flour (plus a little extra for dredging)*

*1 cup hot whole milk*

*¼ pound raw shrimp, cooked in the shell, then shelled, cleaned, and chopped*

*Pinch of grated nutmeg*

*Salt and pepper to taste*

*2 eggs, lightly beaten*

*1 cup breadcrumbs*

*Vegetable oil for frying*

Over a low flame, heat the oil in a saucepan. Add the chopped onion and serrano chile. Sauté until the onion is translucent, but do not allow it to brown. Add ¼ cup flour and incorporate into oil/vegetable mixture, but do not overcook. Whisk in the milk until the mixture comes to a boil. Continue to whisk until the mixture thickens. Add the chopped, cooked shrimp and seasonings. Cook for another minute. Remove from heat and put the mixture in a bowl to cool.

Shape a teaspoonful of the mixture into a bite-size ball and roll lightly in remaining flour. Then dip in the beaten egg to coat and roll each ball in breadcrumbs. Continue until you have made balls of all of the shrimp mixture. Set aside to dry.

Pour ½ inch of oil into a frying pan or cast iron skillet and heat over medium-high heat until the oil shimmers. Fry the croquettes until they are golden brown. Using a slotted spoon, remove them as they are done and drain on paper towels. Makes 24 croquettes.

# MASA SOPES

## Cornmeal Boats

These little handmade masa boats are an all-purpose base for savory appetizers. You can top them with Guacamole, Cochinita Pibil, the filling for Enchilada Suizas de Jaiba, grilled shrimp, or Salsa Mexicana and a sprinkling of cheese. The little boats themselves can be made ahead and frozen. It never hurts to have a bag of them in the freezer to thaw out and top for a quick appetizer.

*2 tablespoons vegetable shortening or lard*

*⅓ cup all-purpose flour*

*1 teaspoon baking powder*

*1 teaspoon sea salt*

*2¼ cups masa harina*

*1½ cups hot water*

*Vegetable oil for frying*

In a mixing bowl, combine all ingredients except the oil, knead, cover, and set it aside to rest for about 30 minutes. Divide the dough into 24 balls. Flatten each ball into a circle or oval about ¾ inch thick. On lightly greased comal or griddle over medium heat, cook the patties about 2 minutes on each side; remove from the comal. When they are cool enough to handle, pinch around the edges to form a little cup or "boat." They can be cooled and frozen at this point. When ready to serve, heat 1 inch of oil in a heavy, cast-iron skillet over medium heat and fry the *sopes* until golden. Drain on paper towels and fill with your choice of savory filling. Serves 6 (3 or 4 per person).

# MOJITOS
## Rum and Mint Cocktail

Caribbean libations are all the rage these days, and the Fonda San Miguel bar is the perfect place to relax with a refreshingly minty Mojito, which originated in Havana. According to San Miguel's bartenders, the successful Mojito is all in how you muddle (mash together) and shake it. Muddling releases the essential oils in the mint and limes and begins to dissolve the sugar.

*1 heaping tablespoon superfine sugar*
*8 fresh mint leaves*
*2 or 3 lime wedges*
*1¼ ounces light rum*
*Crushed ice*
*Club soda*
*Sprig of mint for garnish*
*Sugar cane strip*

Combine sugar, mint leaves, and lime wedges in a tall glass and muddle with a cocktail spoon or the handle of a wooden spoon. Add the rum and fill the glass with crushed ice. Top with a cocktail shaker and shake to a Latin beat. Pour the mixture into a fresh glass, add a splash of club soda, and stir gently. Garnish with fresh mint and a long, thin strip of sugar cane, cut to look like a straw. Serves 1.

## Variation

For a Raspberry Mojito, muddle 4 or 5 fresh raspberries with the sugar, mint leaves, and lime wedges. If desired, substitute a raspberry-flavored rum for the light rum and garnish with a several additional fresh raspberries.

# FRESH LIME MARGARITAS

Margaritas and Mexican food are a classic combination. Fresh lime margaritas have been a trademark of Fonda San Miguel since the day it opened, and they remain so today. In the early years, bartender Tom Hess would come in early to hand-squeeze limes for that evening's shift. For the most authentic results, use the best fresh lime juice you can find.

> *5 lime wedges*
>
> *Coarse salt*
>
> *1 cup silver tequila*
>
> *½ cup Cointreau*
>
> *½ cup fresh lime juice*
>
> *Splash of simple bar syrup, if desired (1 part sugar to 2 parts water, boiled 5 minutes)*
>
> *Ice cubes*

Rub one of the lime wedges around the rim of 4 martini glasses, dip the rims in coarse salt, and set aside. Combine tequila, Cointreau, lime juice, and syrup in a shaker and add a handful of ice cubes. Shake well and strain into the prepared glasses. Garnish each glass with the remaining lime wedges. Serves 4.

# SILVER COIN MARGARITA

Miguel spent two years as executive chef at one of the Zócalo restaurants in New York City and brought this delightful cocktail back to Texas with him. Each bartender at Fonda San Miguel has his own personal twist on the final preparation of this drink, but only the basic version is included here. You may want to vary the amount of lime juice, depending on the sweetness of the watermelon-infused tequila. Be sure to use the ripest, sweetest watermelon you can find, and your summer party guests will be very impressed. The infusion will keep for several days in the refrigerator.

> *1½ ounces watermelon-infused tequila (see below)*
>
> *¾ ounce Cointreau*
>
> *⅓ ounce fresh lime juice*
>
> *Crushed ice*
>
> *Wedge of watermelon rind for garnish*

### Watermelon-Infused Tequila

Makes about 3 quarts.

> *Half of a 12-pound watermelon, cut into chunks (about 8 cups)*
>
> *1 1-liter bottle Herradura Silver Tequila*

Prepare the watermelon-infused tequila. Combine watermelon chunks and tequila in a 1½- to 2-gallon non-reactive container and use a whisk or potato masher to break up the fruit. Cover and refrigerate for 48 hours. Push the mixture through a fine sieve, pressing on the watermelon to extract all the juice. Dispose of the pulp and seeds.

To prepare the cocktail, combine the watermelon-infused tequila, Cointreau, and lime juice in a cocktail shaker with a handful of crushed ice. Shake and strain into a glass. Serve straight up, garnished with a wedge of watermelon rind. Serves 1.

# MANGO MARGARITAS

Brilliant orange in color, mango margaritas are a very popular libation at the Fonda San Miguel bar, especially at the Hacienda Sunday Brunch Buffet, where they are often ordered by the pitcher. In lieu of fresh or canned mangoes, you can also substitute a good-quality mango sorbet for the mangoes, sugar, and crushed ice.

> *¾ cup fresh lime juice*
>
> *5 tablespoons superfine sugar*
>
> *2 ripe fresh mangoes, peeled, pitted, and chopped, or 2 cups canned mangoes, well-drained* ✿
>
> *¾ cup tequila*
>
> *1½ ounces Triple Sec*
>
> *Crushed ice*

Combine the lime juice and sugar in a nonreactive pitcher and stir until the sugar is dissolved. Puree the mangoes in a blender. Add tequila, Triple Sec, lime juice mixture, and a little of the crushed ice and blend until smooth. Pour the mixture into the pitcher and serve immediately over crushed ice. Makes about 1 quart.

# PALOMA

## Grapefruit Soda Margarita

In the summer of 2004, while attending a restaurant show in Mexico City, Tom took the opportunity to visit one of his favorite restaurants, Fonda El Refugio, one of the oldest, most respected, and most authentic restaurants in the country. It was there that he discovered this refreshing twist on the standard margarita. When he returned home, he made sure that this new libation was added to the Fonda San Miguel bar menu. And it turns out customers like it every bit as much as Tom does. Most Hispanic markets carry the Jarritos brand of soda, but if you absolutely can't find it, you can substitute Fanta or Sprite, though the resulting cocktail won't be quite as good. Once Tom began experimenting with different flavors of Jarritos soda, he came up with some other sure-fire combinations, matching Tamarindo (tamarind) with white rum and Jamaica (hibiscus) with vodka.

> *2 lime wedges*
>
> *Coarse salt*
>
> *Crushed ice*
>
> *1¼ ounces silver tequila*
>
> *1 13.5-ounce bottle of grapefruit soda*

Moisten the rim of a highball glass with one of the lime wedges and dip the rim in salt. Fill the glass two-thirds full with crushed ice. Add tequila and grapefruit soda, stir lightly, and garnish with the remaining lime wedge. Serves 1.

## Variation

For a Paloma with some heat, add a pinch of chili powder to the coarse salt and proceed as directed.

# SANGRÍA FONDA SAN MIGUEL

When Tom and Miguel invited their longtime friend Lucinda Hutson to share a drink recipe for this book, she wanted to create something special, a libation as colorful and festive as Fonda San Miguel itself! Lucinda suggests serving this punch from a large lidded glass jar like the ones used on the streets of Mexico for *aguas frescas* (fresh-fruit punches). The dried hibiscus flowers give this punch its tartness and color. A bright yellow liqueur from Mexico called Damiana adds an exotic herbaceous flavor. It is made from a wild yellow-flowered herb that is native to Baja California. There, Mexicans use Damiana instead of Cointreau to flavor margaritas. The liqueur comes in a bottle shaped like a curvaceous woman and is reputedly an aphrodisiac. When you add it to Lucinda's sangría, watch out!

*1 1.5-liter bottle of Spanish or Chilean dry, fruity red wine, such as Cousino-Macul Cabernet Sauvignon (Chile)*

*2 cups Presidente brandy*

*1 cup Damiana liqueur or additional to taste*

*1 small pineapple, peeled, cored, and cut into bite-size chunks*

*5 Valencia oranges, halved and sliced*

*1 teaspoon Mexican vanilla extract* ❀

*¾ cup dried hibiscus flowers*

*1 3-inch Mexican cinnamon stick* ❀

*1 pound fresh strawberries with hulls*

*3 lemons, sliced*

*3 limes, sliced*

*1 16-ounce package frozen cubed mangoes or peaches*

*Squirt, sparkling wine, or champagne to taste (or substitute Sprite)*

*Assorted fresh fruit for garnish*

*Mint springs for garnish*

In a large jar, combine wine, brandy, and liqueur. Add the pineapple, oranges, vanilla, hibiscus flowers, and cinnamon stick. Refrigerate for 24 to 48 hours. A few hours before serving, add the fresh strawberries, lemons, and limes. Directly before serving, add the frozen mangoes, which will serve as ice. Serve in glasses garnished with fresh fruit and mint sprigs with a big splash of Squirt. Makes about 1 gallon.

# RED SANGRÍA

This traditional wine punch presents the opportunity to turn robust jug wine and fresh seasonal fruits into a festive party drink. The recipe includes a mix of firm fruits (such as seedless grapes, apple slices, and pear slices) and soft fruits (like strawberries, peaches, and kiwi). The soft fruits are added to the glasses at serving time.

*2 oranges, thinly sliced*

*1 lemon, thinly sliced*

*1 lime, thinly sliced*

*4 cups fresh firm fruits, prepared and sliced as appropriate*

*1 gallon full-bodied dry red wine, such as Cabernet Sauvignon*

*1½ to 2 cups orange liqueur, such as Cointreau or Triple Sec*

*1½ cups Presidente brandy*

*2 bunches lemon verbena, washed and stemmed (about 2 cups)*

*Fresh soft fruits, prepared and sliced as appropriate*

*Club soda, champagne, or sparkling wine*

Combine citrus slices and other firm fruits in a large, nonreactive container. Add wine, liqueur, brandy, and lemon verbena. Cover and refrigerate overnight (or up to 3 days). When ready to serve, put some soft fruits into each wine glass and fill two-thirds full with the sangría. Top off with a splash of club soda. Makes 6 to 7 quarts.

# CAZUELA GUADALAJARA
## Tropical Tequila Punch

The James Beard House in New York City honored Fonda San Miguel with an invitation to present a lavish Mexican meal there in 1995. Tom included nationally celebrated food and garden writer and tequila aficionada Lucinda Hutson in the festivities, and she served some of her tequila specialties. Cazuela Guadalajara was a big hit. (A variation of this recipe appears in her book *¡Viva Tequila! Cocktails, Cooking, and Other Agave Adventures*.) She served it from a five-gallon glass jar that showed off the premium tequila and all the tropical fruits within. The ultimate fruit cocktail, so to speak!

> Half of a 12- to 16-pound watermelon, cut into bite-size chunks or triangles (about 8 cups)
>
> 1 small pineapple, peeled, cored, and cut into bite-size chunks
>
> 1 1-liter bottle of silver tequila
>
> 2 cups gold tequila
>
> 4 oranges, cut into wedges
>
> 2 lemons, sliced
>
> 3 star fruit, cut into star-shaped slices
>
> ½ cup lime juice
>
> 4 cups orange juice
>
> 1 46-ounce can unsweetened pineapple juice
>
> 6 limes, quartered
>
> 3 small ruby grapefruit, cut into wedges
>
> Cracked ice
>
> 3 12-ounce cans Squirt or other citrus-flavored soda

Combine watermelon and pineapple chunks in a 2-gallon, wide-mouth glass jar. Add the tequilas, oranges, lemons, star fruit, and juices. Refrigerate for 6 to 8 hours, stirring occasionally. A few hours before serving, add the limes and grapefruit. Serve in wide-mouth glasses or bowls filled with cracked ice, a generous splash of Squirt, and a straw. Makes 6 to 7 quarts.

*NOTE*: The flavor of this punch improves with age. It will keep several days in the refrigerator, although the watermelon will lose its texture. Add more fruit if desired.

## Danny Brennan

*Zapata*, 1974. Oil on canvas, 40 × 36 inches.

*This painting of the great revolutionary Emiliano Zapata is the very first painting I purchased for Fonda San Miguel—about 1975 or early 1976. The restaurant has since acquired a number of additional paintings by Danny Brennan, and they're all very Gauguin-like. But this first one seems to dominate—a lot of people like it and constantly refer to it. In fact, one of our customers, Austin screenwriter and producer Bill Wittliff, wants to buy it every time he comes in. I once made the comment that I would never have expected a firebrand like Zapata to dress like such a dandy: in a pink suit and tie, holding a cigar. Wittliff said, "Oh, yes, he loved to dress up." He plans to write a screenplay for a movie about Zapata one of these days. What's interesting is that I bought the painting from Gallery San Miguel in San Miguel de Allende, and here it is in a restaurant called Fonda San Miguel. Although not Mexican, the artist lived in Mexico for quite a few years—in San Miguel and also in Puerto Vallarta. I carried this painting under my arm on the train from San Miguel to Laredo.*

*T.G.*

# AGUA DE SANDÍA
## Watermelon

*Aguas frescas*, literally "fresh waters," are a popular drink all over Mexico, where you'll often find them served from large glass jars on the counters of food stalls and cafes. There are as many different varieties as there are tropical fruits. Some of the most popular flavors are made from tamarind pods, dried hibiscus flowers, and refreshing cucumbers with lime and a little chile. A good blender is needed to puree the fruit. Traditionally, *aguas frescas* are the texture of lemonade rather than that of the more American smoothie. These refreshing drinks look best when served from a large pitcher, punch bowl, or clear glass drink dispenser. Garnished with fresh-cut fruit and mint leaves, a punch bowl full of *agua fresca* is a wonderful addition to any breakfast, brunch, or party buffet.

*1 12- to 15-pound watermelon, seeded and cut into chunks, with any juice reserved (about 8 to 12 cups)*

*6 to 8 cups water*

*¼ to ½ cup sugar or to taste*

Working in batches, puree watermelon chunks in a blender with the reserved juice and 1 to 2 cups of the water. Push puree through a fine sieve. Transfer liquid to a large pitcher and stir in sugar and the remaining water. Stir well to dissolve sugar. Refrigerate. Serve chilled over ice. Makes 2½ to 3 quarts.

# AGUA DE PIÑA
## Pineapple

Tart and refreshing, this pineapple drink is also loaded with healthy vitamin C.

*1 large pineapple, peeled, cored, and cut into chunks, with any juice reserved*

*3 to 4 cups water*

*4 tablespoons sugar or to taste*

Working in batches, puree pineapple chunks in a blender with the reserved juice and 1 to 2 cups of the water. Transfer liquid to a large pitcher and stir in sugar and the remaining water. Stir well to dissolve sugar. Refrigerate. Serve chilled over ice. Makes 1½ to 2 quarts.

# AGUA DE JAMAICA
## Hibiscus

The burgundy-colored dried calyx of the hibiscus flower, *flor de Jamaica*, is the main ingredient in this *agua fresca*.

*3 ounces dried hibiscus flowers*

*8 cups water*

*⅓ to ½ cup sugar or to taste*

In a 3-quart nonreactive saucepan, combine dried hibiscus flowers with water and bring to a boil. Remove from heat, cover, and allow to steep at least 24 hours. Strain liquid through a fine sieve into a pitcher, pressing down on the flowers to extract all the liquid. Add sugar and stir well. Refrigerate. Serve chilled over ice. Makes 2 quarts.

José Fors

*El chile*, 2000. Oil on canvas, 39 × 47½ inches.

A favorite of mine is this painting by José Fors in two parts, with its ambiguous arm on the left reaching out for a red chile on the far right. It's absolutely one of the restaurant's most stunning paintings—when people walk by and see it, they just have to stop and look. It's not to everybody's taste, but I think it's pretty wonderful. I bought it from the late Dana Ravel, who ran Galerie Ravel in Austin for many years. She was one of my dearest friends, and she had a keen eye, particularly for Mexican and South American artists. Galerie Ravel was one of the leading galleries in the United States. I bought this painting from Dana at a show that she held for José Fors. A Cuban by birth, Fors now lives in Guadalajara with his Mexican wife and has shows from time to time. Like many Cubans, he left Cuba and came to the United States, lived in Miami, and then eventually moved to Mexico. He is primarily a musician—he has his own band, writes his own music, and records his own CDs. Then he started painting, and it has been his creative focus for a number of years. He's a very intense painter—this is one of his more benign pieces. We also have another painting of his, Frutas.

T.G.

# ENSALADAS

Salads

The salad component of Mexican cuisine is a cornucopia of New World tropical fruits, greens, herbs, and vegetables, paired with the best ingredients transplanted from Europe. The bountiful array of salads presented at Fonda San Miguel is a perfect example of this delicious diversity—rich, buttery guacamole; tangy, astringent nopal cactus; crunchy jícama with fruit, chile, and cilantro; greens with beets and pomegranates; zesty pickled vegetables . . . The possibilities are endless.

# ENSALADA DE NOPALITOS
## Fonda San Miguel Steamed Nopales

Many people ask how we make our nopales (strips of cactus paddles) because they taste so much better than the ones you buy in a jar. We make them fresh! They're available from many markets, cleaned and ready to use. We cook them *al vapor* (steamed) so they retain all of their natural vitamins. After steaming, nopales are delicious in salads, served with egg dishes, and in many other recipes that call for them.

*4 tablespoons olive oil*

*3 tablespoons white onion, finely chopped*

*2 garlic cloves, minced*

*3½ cups cactus paddles, cleaned and cut into 2-inch strips*

*Salt to taste*

In a cast iron skillet, heat oil over medium-high heat until it shimmers. Add onions and garlic and sauté for about 30 seconds. Add the cactus strips, making sure they do not stick to the pan. Stir constantly and gently with a wooden spoon. Cover and reduce the heat to low. Keep covered for about 10 minutes, giving the nopales time to change color and release their juices. Remove the cover and cook over medium heat until the nopales reabsorb their juices, about 8 to 10 minutes. Salt to taste.

## To Prepare a Salad of Nopales

*3½ cups (1 pound) nopales*

*8 sprigs cilantro, chopped*

*Half of a medium white onion, finely chopped*

*2 large tomatoes, seeded and chopped*

*3–4 jalapeño en escabeche (pickled), chopped*

*4 teaspoons pickling juice from the jalapeño can*

*¼ cup shredded panela cheese*

In a nonreactive bowl, mix together all ingredients EXCEPT the cheese. Set aside at room temperature for 45 minutes to allow the flavors to meld. Serve on a bed of lettuce with blue corn tortilla strips (optional), and garnish with the cheese. Serves 6.

# ENSALADA DE JÍCAMA CON MELÓN
## Jícama-Melon Salad

Although many fresh condiments in Mexican cuisine are called *pico de gallo* ("rooster's beak"), this refreshing salad from the Mexican state of Jalisco is also known as Pico de Gallo. Depending on the seasonal availability of fresh fruit, Miguel has found that the salad is equally good made with Rio Star grapefruit, pineapple, blood oranges, cantaloupe, watermelon, and honeydew melon. The contrast of sweet fruit, crunchy jícama, tangy lime juice, and a little dash of chili powder makes for a delightful palate cleanser. A popular item on the Hacienda Buffet, it can be tossed with Pomegranate Dressing, the dressing for Ensalada de Noche Buena, as pictured.

*1 large jícama, peeled and cut into ¼-inch-wide strips*

*3 navel oranges, peeled and sectioned with pulp and membrane removed*

*1 large cantaloupe or honeydew melon, peeled, seeded, and cut into bite-size chunks*

*½ cup pomegranate seeds*

*1 cup fresh lime juice*

*2 sprigs cilantro, chopped*

*1 teaspoon sea salt*

*½ teaspoon chili powder (optional)*

In a nonreactive bowl, combine jícama and fruit. Toss with lime juice, cilantro, and salt. Refrigerate about 1 hour to allow flavors to meld. Toss with chili powder before serving. Serves 6.

# ENSALADA DE NOCHEBUENA
## Christmas Eve Salad

When Miguel was growing up in Phoenix, his grandmother grew pomegranates and citrus fruits in her yard, and those fruits usually found their way into her cooking. This is her version of a traditional salad eaten during the Christmas season when the pomegranates and other ingredients are available. The bright colors make a brilliant presentation on the holiday table.

*6 medium beets, peeled, cooked, and diced (optional)*
*4 oranges, peeled and sectioned, with membranes removed*
*4 Red Delicious apples, peeled, cored, and diced*
*1 medium jícama, peeled and cut into matchstick strips*
*1 cup roasted unsalted peanuts*
*4 tablespoons sugar*
*¼ cup rice vinegar*
*2 tablespoons olive oil*
*¾ cup club soda*
*1 cup fresh pineapple cubes*
*2 bananas, sliced*
*1 head iceberg lettuce, thinly sliced*

## Pomegranate Dressing
Makes 1½ cups.

*Seeds of 1 whole pomegranate, with some seeds reserved for garnish*
*½ cup sour cream*
*4 tablespoons sugar*
*½ cup apple juice*

Combine all salad ingredients except the lettuce in a large nonreactive bowl and refrigerate for at least 2 to 3 hours.

While the salad is chilling, make the Pomegranate Dressing. Combine the pomegranate seeds, sour cream, sugar, and apple juice in a blender and puree.

Drain the salad and toss with Pomegranate Dressing. Serve on a bed of iceberg lettuce and garnish with reserved pomegranate seeds. Serves 8 to 10.

# ENSALADA DE ESPINACAS
## Spinach Salad

Renowned cooking instructor and cookbook author María Dolores Torres Yzabal of Mexico City is a good friend of both Tom Gilliland and chef Roberto Santibáñez. Roberto adapted this recipe for spinach salad from her lovely book *The Mexican Gourmet,* written with Shelton Wiseman. The salad appears on both the dinner menu and the Hacienda Sunday Brunch Buffet at Fonda San Miguel.

*6 cups baby spinach leaves, washed, stemmed, and torn into bite-size pieces*

*1 teaspoon plus 1 tablespoon safflower oil*

*¼ cup blanched almond slices*

*2 corn tortillas, cut into small squares*

*1 pasilla chile, thinly sliced* ✿

*2 cups panela cheese, cut into ½-inch cubes* ✿

*3 tablespoons sesame seeds, toasted*

## Spinach Salad Dressing
Makes ⅓ cup.

*1 tablespoon apple cider vinegar*

*1 tablespoon shredded white onion*

*Pinch of sea salt and ground black pepper*

*3 tablespoons safflower oil*

Put spinach in a large nonreactive bowl and set aside. Heat 1 teaspoon of the oil in a small skillet over medium heat and fry almonds until golden brown, being careful not to burn them, about 2 minutes. Remove with a slotted spoon and drain on paper towels. Add the remaining 1 tablespoon oil and fry the tortilla squares until crisp and golden, about 1 to 2 minutes. Remove and drain on paper towels. Fry the chile slices 10 to 15 seconds, being careful not to burn them; remove and drain on paper towels. Toss the almonds, tortillas, and chiles with the spinach.

To prepare the dressing, combine vinegar, onion, salt, and pepper in a small nonreactive bowl. Add oil in a steady stream, whisking constantly.

Toss the salad with the dressing and garnish with cheese cubes and sesame seeds. Serve immediately. Serves 6 to 8.

## Noe Katz

*Escaleras y serpientes*, 1998. Oil on canvas, 35 × 40 inches.

*Noe Katz is a well-known artist from Mexico City whose paintings are so popular, especially in Japan, that he frequently sells out of his works at shows. Sometimes people are so eager for his work that they will buy it sight unseen. I purchased this fascinating painting with lots of greens and blues from Dana Ravel, who was very instrumental in helping the restaurant acquire some of its better pieces. Escaleras y serpientes is very contemporary and what I call a "walk stopper." In selecting art for Fonda San Miguel, I've always wanted to show the great diversity of Mexican art—from the more traditional to the most contemporary. Mexico is a country that honors and treasures its artists. The museums are always full, and people from all walks of life love art.*

T.G.

# SALPICÓN DE RES
## Shredded Beef Salad

A *salpicón* is a concoction of shredded meat dressed in a savory dressing, traditionally made with vinegar as a preservative. This beef salad is rich in flavor, smoke, and spice. It makes a delicious luncheon dish when served on a bed of shredded greens, and can also be used as a topping for *sopes* or tostadas. It's possible to make a milder version by first seeding the chipotle chiles or simply using fewer of them.

> *3 pounds flank or skirt steak, cut into 2-inch cubes*
> *2 medium white onions, cut into quarters*
> *10 whole black peppercorns*
> *3 bay leaves*
> *4 garlic cloves*
> *2 teaspoons sea salt*
> *Shredded leaf lettuce*
> *4 or 5 medium tomatoes, cut into 18 slices*
> *2 large avocados, peeled, pitted, and cut into 18 slices*
> *6 tablespoons shredded panela cheese or other dry Mexican cheese* ❈
> *Corn tortilla chips*

## Dressing for Salpicón de Res
Makes 2 to 2½ cups.

> *½ cup olive oil*
> *1 cup apple cider vinegar*
> *4 chipotle chiles in adobo sauce, chopped* ❈
> *2 tablespoons adobo sauce from the can*
> *Juice of 2 limes*
> *Juice of 2 oranges*
> *2 teaspoons ground black pepper*
> *½ cup firmly packed cilantro leaves, chopped*
> *Sea salt to taste*

Place meat, onions, and seasonings in a stock pot and cover with water. Bring to a boil. Reduce heat to low and simmer for about 25 minutes, or until meat is done. Remove from heat and drain, discarding cooking liquid. When meat is cool enough to handle, shred by hand or with two forks. Set aside while preparing the dressing.

Combine the dressing ingredients in a nonreactive bowl; whisk to blend well. Toss dressing with the shredded beef. Set aside at room temperature to allow flavors to blend, about 30 minutes. Arrange beef on a bed of shredded lettuce and garnish with slices of tomato and avocado and the shredded cheese. Serve with tortilla chips. Serves 6.

# GUACAMOLE

What would a Mexican meal be without guacamole? It goes with everything! Just be sure to always use knobby black Hass avocados from either Mexico or California—the green variety from Florida doesn't make the smooth, creamy sauce you want for your family and guests.

> *2 ripe avocados, as large as possible*
>
> *1 large tomato, chopped and drained*
>
> *¼ white onion, peeled and minced*
>
> *2 tablespoons chopped fresh cilantro leaves*
>
> *2 serrano chiles, minced (or to taste)*
>
> *1 tablespoon freshly squeezed lime juice (preferably from small, round Mexican limes)*
>
> *Sea salt to taste*

Cut the avocados in half. Tap the pit with the sharp blade of a knife and twist to remove the pit. Scoop out the pulp with a spoon and mash in a *molcajete* or nonreactive bowl. Add the tomato, onion, cilantro, chiles, and lime juice. Stir with a wooden spoon. Season with sea salt to taste. Serve immediately. Serves 6.

# ENSALADA DE TRES CHILES
## Three-Pepper Slaw

In 1998 Miguel collaborated with cookbook author Marilyn Tausend on the cookbook *Cocina de la Familia*, winner of an award from the prestigious International Association of Culinary Professionals. A recipe from that book inspired this crunchy, colorful, three-pepper slaw. In the age-old barbecue tradition, Miguel serves the slaw with Agujas de Res, his delicious Yucatan-style barbecued short ribs. The salad is an excellent accompaniment to beef or pork barbecue as well as grilled fish.

> *4 cups shredded cabbage*
>
> *2 cups jícama (1 to 1½ pounds), peeled and cut into matchstick strips*
>
> *½ cup olive oil*
>
> *1 small white onion, finely chopped*
>
> *1 red bell pepper, seeded and cut into matchstick strips*
>
> *1 yellow bell pepper, seeded and cut into matchstick strips*
>
> *1 poblano chile, roasted, peeled, seeded, and sliced into ¼-inch strips* ✽
>
> *½ teaspoon dried Mexican oregano*
>
> *⅓ cup apple cider vinegar*
>
> *1½ tablespoons sugar*
>
> *½ teaspoon sea salt*

Combine cabbage and jícama in a large nonreactive salad bowl; set aside. Heat olive oil in a medium skillet over medium heat and add onion, peppers, chile, and oregano. Sauté for about 3 minutes, or until vegetables are wilted. Add vinegar and sugar and bring mixture to a simmer. Remove from heat and set aside to cool for 3 to 5 minutes. While mixture is still warm, pour over the cabbage and jícama; toss well. Sprinkle with sea salt and toss again. Refrigerate for at least 1 hour to allow flavors to blend.

# CILANTRO-BASIL DRESSING

Mexican culinary consultant Patricia Quintana is a longtime friend of the restaurant, and this delicious salad dressing is one of her creations. At Fonda San Miguel it is used to dress both the house salad and a delicate late-spring salad of squash blossoms.

*½ cup apple cider vinegar*
*½ cup vegetable oil*
*½ cup olive oil*
*2 garlic cloves, peeled*
*½ cup firmly packed cilantro leaves*
*½ cup firmly packed basil leaves*
*1½ teaspoons sugar*
*½ teaspoon ground black pepper*
*Sea salt to taste*

Combine all ingredients in a large blender and blend for about 3 minutes, or until mixture is smooth. Refrigerate until ready to use. The mixture can be blended again if it separates. Makes 2 cups.

# AVOCADO CREAM DRESSING

This voluptuous dressing is good on leafy greens as well as on a composed salad of avocados and grapefruit slices.

*2 tablespoons mayonnaise*
*5 garlic cloves, chopped*
*¼ cup chopped white onion*
*1 tablespoon fresh lime juice*
*½ teaspoon dried thyme*
*¼ teaspoon sea salt*
*¼ teaspoon ground black pepper*
*1 whole bay leaf, crumbled*
*Half of a ripe avocado, peeled and pitted*
*½ cup water*
*1 cup corn oil*

Combine all ingredients except the corn oil in a heavy-duty blender. Puree until smooth. With the motor running, add the oil in a thin stream until the mixture forms an emulsion, about 2 minutes. Remove from the blender and chill. The mixture can be blended again if it separates. Makes 2 cups.

SOPAS

Soups

The very early buzz about Fonda San Miguel had to do with a unique and delicate corn soup garnished with roasted chiles and crunchy tortilla pieces. Inspired by a Diana Kennedy recipe, Sopa de Elote was to become the restaurant's first signature dish. The vegetarian clientele was particularly wild about it, and the soup developed a solid following that remains faithful to this day. A rich and fragrant tortilla soup soon followed, and then Miguel began to augment the menu with some of his grandmother's soup recipes, the comfort foods of his Phoenix childhood.

# POZOLE ESTILO JALISCO
## Pozole Jalisco Style

Jalisco is famous for its red pozole and this delicious soup is both flavorful and filling. It's typically served with crisp, plain tostadas: ungarnished baked or fried tortillas.

### For the Pozole

1¼ pounds boneless pork shoulder, fat removed

5 cups chicken broth (see separate recipe)

6 whole guajillo chiles, stems removed

1 white onion, peeled and chopped

4 garlic cloves, peeled and flattened

2 bay leaves

1 sprig fresh thyme

Sea salt to taste

1 15-ounce can of white hominy, drained

### For the Garnish

¼ head green cabbage, finely shredded

½ cup white onion, finely chopped

2 tablespoons dried Mexican oregano

1 tablespoon crushed chile de árbol

10 radishes, thinly sliced

Lime wedges

Put the whole piece of boneless pork shoulder in a large pot. Add the chicken broth, guajillo chiles, onion, garlic, bay leaves, and thyme. Cook over medium heat for approximately 25 to 30 minutes until the meat is tender. Add salt and correct if necessary. Remove and discard the chiles, bay leaves, and garlic. Remove the pork shoulder from the pot and roughly shred it with the meat's grain. Return the meat to the pot and add hominy, drained of its water. Simmer on low heat until the pozole is hot.

Serve the pozole in large heated bowls. Serve condiments in separate bowls so that each diner may add according to taste. Serve with tostadas. Serves 8 to 10.

# SOPA DE ELOTE ❁
## Corn Soup

Corn is the very foundation of Mexican culture and cuisine. This wonderful soup is adapted from a recipe presented by Diana Kennedy in her influential first cookbook, *The Cuisines of Mexico*. As the original menu consultant for Fonda San Miguel, she shared many of her well-researched, authentic recipes with Miguel. Corn soup was one of the first breakout dishes to create a following within the restaurant, and it has maintained its popularity. It is even copied now at other Mexican restaurants in Austin. At the height of summer, this soup is marvelous, made with corn cut off the cob. The second choice is frozen corn. *Never use canned corn.*

4 cups fresh corn kernels, cut and scraped from 5 or 6 ears of corn, or about 2 10-ounce packages of frozen corn kernels, thawed

4½ cups milk

¼ cup butter, softened

1 teaspoon sea salt

2 poblano chiles, roasted, peeled, seeded, and diced ❁

6 tablespoons shredded Monterey Jack cheese

6 corn tortillas, cut into thin strips and fried crisp

Combine corn and 1 cup of the milk in a blender. Puree at high speed until smooth; set aside. In a heavy, 3-quart nonreactive stock pot, heat the butter over medium heat until melted and bubbly. Add the corn puree and cook over medium heat for about 5 minutes, stirring constantly. Add the remaining 3½ cups milk and the salt; bring mixture to a boil. Reduce heat to low and simmer for about 15 minutes, stirring to avoid sticking. In each of 6 warm soup bowls, put 1 tablespoon each of the diced chiles and shredded cheese. Ladle the hot soup into the bowls and garnish with a few tortilla strips. Serves 6.

# SOPA TARASCA TIPO CONDE ❧
## Tarascan Bean and Tomato Soup

This hearty soup is a dish native to the indigenous Purépecha, also known as the Tarascan Indians, who live in the region near Morelia, Michoacan. It is a great restorative and sometimes appears as a special on Fonda San Miguel's dinner menu during the winter months.

> 4 cups canned pinto beans with ½ to ¾ cup of their own juice
>
> 2 medium tomatoes, broiled ✽
>
> 1 garlic clove
>
> Quarter of a medium white onion, chopped
>
> 3 tablespoons vegetable oil or lard
>
> 2½ cups Basic Chicken Broth ❖
>
> Sea salt to taste
>
> 6 tablespoons corn oil
>
> 2 corn tortillas, cut into ¼-inch strips
>
> 2 pasilla chiles, seeded ✽
>
> ¾ cup shredded panela cheese
>
> ½ cup sour cream

Put beans and bean juice in a blender and blend to a puree. Transfer to a bowl and set aside. Combine tomatoes (skins on), garlic, and onion in the blender and puree. In a large, heavy stock pot or Dutch oven, heat the vegetable oil over high heat. Add the tomato puree and cook for about 7 minutes. Add the bean puree, reduce heat to medium, and cook an additional 8 minutes, stirring often. Add the chicken broth, reduce heat to low, and cook an additional 10 minutes. Check seasoning, adding salt if necessary.

    While soup is cooking, heat the corn oil in a small, heavy skillet over medium heat. Add the tortilla strips and fry until crisp and golden, about 2 to 3 minutes. Remove with a slotted spoon and drain on paper towels. Fry the chiles in the same oil for about 10 seconds each, or until they puff up. Remove with a slotted spoon and drain on paper towels; allow to cool a little and then crumble. Put 2 tablespoons of the shredded cheese in each of 6 soup bowls. Ladle the hot soup into the bowls and garnish with the fried tortillas strips, crumbled chiles, and 1 tablespoon of the sour cream. Serves 6.

# SOPA DE ALBÓNDIGAS
## Meatball Soup

Hearty meatball soup makes a very satisfying meal when paired with crusty bolillos or fresh hot tortillas. This heirloom recipe comes from Miguel's mother, Amelia Velásquez Galbraith, and it is one of his favorite comfort foods. It sometimes appears as a special on the Fonda San Miguel dinner menu.

*1 pound ground beef*

*1 pound ground pork*

*Half of a medium white onion, chopped*

*2 eggs*

*½ teaspoon dried Mexican oregano*

*1½ teaspoons sea salt*

*1 teaspoon ground black pepper*

*½ cup unseasoned breadcrumbs*

### Broth

*2 quarts chicken or beef broth*

*1 large white onion, chopped*

*4 garlic cloves, minced*

*2 canned Anaheim chiles, chopped*

*2 large tomatoes, chopped*

*¼ cup uncooked rice*

*1 8-ounce can tomato sauce*

*½ cup chopped cilantro leaves*

In a mixing bowl combine beef and pork; set aside. Combine onion, eggs, oregano, salt, and pepper in a blender and mix. Pour into the meat mixture. Add the bread crumbs and work the mixture together with your hands until everything is incorporated. Make 24 1-inch meatballs, cover, and set aside.

To make the broth, combine all broth ingredients in a 4-quart, nonreactive stock pot. Bring to a boil, reduce heat to medium, and simmer for 15 minutes. Carefully drop meatballs into the hot broth, one at a time. Cover and cook for about 30 minutes, or until meatballs are cooked through. Serves 6.

# MENUDO BLANCO
## Tripe Soup

In Mexican folk wisdom, menudo is widely known as a restorative and a sure-fire hangover cure. Many variations can be found across Mexico and the southwestern United States. This particular recipe comes from Miguel's grandmother, who was born in the Mexican state of Sonora and spent most of her life in Arizona.

*2 pounds honeycomb tripe, cut into small squares*

*1 medium white onion, chopped*

*3 cloves garlic*

*10 whole black peppercorns*

*2 teaspoons sea salt*

*4 quarts water*

*2 15.5-ounce cans hominy, drained*

*1 bunch green onions, chopped, including green tops*

*1 tablespoon dried Mexican oregano*

*½ cup chopped cilantro leaves*

*6 serrano chiles, chopped* ✽

Combine tripe, onion, garlic, peppercorns, and salt in an 8- to 10-quart stock pot. Add water, bring to a boil, reduce heat to simmer, and cook for 2 hours uncovered. Add hominy and cook over low heat for an additional 30 to 45 minutes. Check seasonings, adding salt if needed. Ladle the hot soup into 8 soup bowls. Garnish with a sprinkling of green onions, Mexican oregano, cilantro, and chiles. Serves 8.

*NOTE*: For a traditional dish, 1 pound of prepared dried hominy, or *nixtamal*, can be substituted for the canned hominy. Just adjust the cooking time by cooking an additional 2 hours after adding the dried hominy.

## Pedro Friedeberg

*Hand-Chair*. Wood, approximately 37 × 18 inches.

*How does one describe surrealist artist Pedro Friedeberg? Genius? Comedian? Eccentric? Born in Italy in 1936 to German-Jewish parents, his family fled early in the war and settled in Mexico. Today, his works are exhibited in museums all over the world and he enjoys an international reputation, but perhaps his own words best capture the contrarian, whimsical nature of this wonderful artist: "I get up at the crack of noon and, after watering my pirañas, I breakfast off things Corinthian. Later in the day I partake in an Ionic lunch followed by a Doric nap. On Tuesdays I sketch a volute or two, and perhaps a pediment, if the mood overtakes me. Wednesday I have set aside for anti-meditation. On Thursdays I usually relax whereas on Friday I write autobiographies." Now that's a routine I can enjoy.*

T.G.

# SOPA SECA DE FIDEOS
## Dry Vermicelli Soup

*Sopa seca,* or "dry soup," is a flavorful pasta dish that is often served in place of rice, especially in the northern states of Mexico. *Fideos* are coils of vermicelli-like pasta. This recipe comes from Miguel's maternal grandmother, Guadalupe Velásquez, a native of Sonora. Miguel remembers that she garnished it with Mexican *crema* and sometimes omitted the chiles when preparing the dish for small children. It is always a hit when Miguel includes it on the Hacienda Sunday Brunch Buffet.

> *1 7-ounce package Mexican* fideo *or vermicelli*
>
> *4 tablespoons safflower oil or other vegetable oil*
>
> *1 medium white onion, chopped*
>
> *2 garlic cloves, minced*
>
> *2 large tomatoes, chopped*
>
> *1 tablespoon chopped cilantro leaves, with 1 teaspoon reserved for garnish*
>
> *4 cups Basic Chicken Broth* ❖
>
> *2 to 4 chipotle chiles in adobo sauce, chopped (optional)* ✳
>
> *Sea salt and ground black pepper to taste*
>
> *½ cup sour cream for garnish*
>
> *½ cup shredded panela cheese for garnish* ✳

In a 4-quart saucepan, heat the oil over medium heat. Break the *fideo* coils into 1-inch pieces and cook until golden brown, about 7 minutes. Add the onion, garlic, tomatoes, and cilantro and cook over medium heat for 2 minutes. Add the chicken broth and chiles. Reduce heat to simmer and cook for about 20 minutes, or until the liquid is absorbed and the pasta is tender. Check seasonings, adding salt and pepper if necessary. Serve on small plates or bowls topped with a tablespoon of sour cream. Sprinkle with the shredded cheese and reserved cilantro. Serves 4 to 6.

# SOPA DE TORTILLA ❋
## Tortilla Soup

The historic restaurant Fonda El Pato in Mexico City was famous for this version of tortilla soup. Customers at Fonda San Miguel are partial to it as well.

*6 tablespoons vegetable oil*

*12 small corn tortillas, cut into ¼-inch strips*

*2 medium tomatoes, broiled ✽*

*¼ cup chopped white onion*

*1 garlic clove*

*6 cups Basic Chicken Broth ❖*

*Sea salt and ground black pepper to taste*

*2 sprigs fresh epazote, chopped, or 2 tablespoons dried epazote ✽*

*6 tablespoons shredded Monterey Jack cheese*

*2 dried pasilla chiles, fried crisp for 10 to 15 seconds, seeded, and crumbled ✽*

Heat oil in a large, heavy Dutch oven over medium heat. Fry tortilla strips until golden brown, about 2 to 3 minutes; remove with a slotted spoon, drain on paper towels, and set aside. Pour off all but 1 tablespoon of the oil in the pan and set aside. In a blender, combine tomatoes, onion, and garlic; puree to a smooth sauce. Heat the remaining tablespoon of oil over medium heat and fry the pureed sauce until it has thickened and is reduced by about one-quarter. Add chicken broth and bring to a boil. Check seasonings, adding salt and pepper if needed. Reduce heat to simmer. Add half of the tortilla strips and the epazote. Cook an additional 5 minutes. To serve, divide the remaining tortilla strips among 6 bowls and put 1 tablespoon of the shredded cheese into each one. Ladle hot soup into the bowls and garnish with crumbled chiles. Serves 6.

## Variation

To make Sopa Azteca, add 2 cups shredded chicken, 1 cup Arroz Mexicano (see "Basic Preparations"), and 1 cup avocado cubes. Garnish with sour cream.

# PLATOS FUERTES

Entrées

In developing dishes for Fonda San Miguel's dinner menu in the early years, Tom and Miguel traveled around Mexico, on their own and with friends such as Diana Kennedy, tasting regional specialties and bringing home ideas to try in the restaurant's kitchen. What has evolved is a menu that features ancient Mexican dishes such as Cochinita Pibil and Pollo en Mole Poblano, taste-tempting tamales and chiles rellenos, robust grilled meats from the northern ranching states, and succulent seafood preparations native to the Mexican Gulf Coast. Although the menu grows and changes, Tom and Miguel maintain a firm commitment to the presentation of authentic regional Mexican cuisine. Tom also believes wholeheartedly that the enjoyment of good Mexican food is enhanced by the consumption of fine wine, so many of the recipes in this section include wine-pairing suggestions.

# CHILES EN NOGADA
## Stuffed Poblano Chiles in Walnut Sauce

When we think of a traditional and emblematic Mexican food, our thoughts may turn to chiles rellenos. Large, shapely, dark green poblano chiles are roasted, peeled, seeded, and stuffed with any number of different fillings: cheese, mashed potato, and tuna fish are commonly used in Mexico. The stuffed chiles are then covered with an egg coating, fried until golden, and served with *caldillo* (a very thin tomato broth).

The most iconic of chiles rellenos is one that many of us outside Mexico have never eaten: it's the *chile en nogada* (stuffed chile in walnut sauce) that is normally eaten in Mexico during August, September, and October, the months when Mexicans celebrate Independence Day and, coincidentally, the months when freshly harvested walnuts and pomegranates are available in the markets.

Legend tells us that *chiles en nogada* were first served in the city of Puebla, Mexico, when Agustín Iturbide arrived to sign a document related to Mexican independence from Spain. The nuns at the Convent of Santa Monica decided to create a new dish to commemorate not only the signing but also Iturbide's birthday on August 28. The dish represents the colors of the newly designed Mexican flag: green, white, and red.

This walnut sauce is one of the glories of the Mexican kitchen. The preparation is time consuming, but this dish is not difficult and it's definitely worth it.

### For the Sauce

*1 cup freshly harvested walnuts, shelled and with the thin brown membrane removed from all nutmeats*

*1 slice French bread soaked in 1 cup whole milk*

*6 ounces full-fat cream cheese*

*1½ cups Mexican table cream (preferable) or sour cream*

*⅛ teaspoon ground cinnamon*

*1 tablespoon sugar*

*¼ cup dry sherry (optional)*

*½ teaspoon salt*

Chop the walnuts and blend until fine in a blender. Add the soaked bread (save the milk) and continue to blend until fairly smooth.

Add the cream cheese, table cream or sour cream, cinnamon, sugar, and dry sherry to the blended mixture and continue to blend. Add the soaking milk a little at a time until the mixture is completely smooth and very creamy.

Serve the sauce at room temperature over the chiles rellenos (use recipe for Chiles Rellenos de Picadillo). The chiles should be served either chilled or at room temperature. Garnish the sauced chiles with chopped parsley and a scattering of deep red pomegranate seeds. Serves 4.

# CHILES ANCHOS RELLENOS DE PICADILLO DE POLLO
## Ancho Chiles Stuffed with Chicken Picadillo

One hallmark of Roberto Santibáñez's years at Fonda San Miguel was the presentation of "off-menu" dinner specials. This unique chile relleno with its distinctive light chicken picadillo was so popular that it became a regular menu item. Arroz Blanco or Frijoles Negros—or both!—are great sides for this dish.

4 cups water

4 ounces piloncillo, grated ✽

½-inch piece of a Mexican cinnamon stick ✽

⅔ cup cider vinegar

½ teaspoon sea salt

8 large ancho chiles, slit open lengthwise, seeded, and deveined ✽

### Picadillo de Pollo

½ cup mild olive oil

Half of a medium white onion, finely chopped (about 1 cup)

2 tablespoons minced garlic

2 pounds Roma tomatoes, finely diced (about 4 cups)

¼ teaspoon dried thyme

2 small bay leaves

¼ cup capers, well rinsed and drained

½ cup pitted Manzanilla olives, chopped

½ cup raisins

2 pounds finely chopped or coarsely ground chicken

1 teaspoon sea salt

½ cup slivered almonds

¼ cup firmly packed cilantro leaves, minced

¼ cup firmly packed parsley leaves, minced

1 tablespoon minced mint leaves

### Cream Sauce for Anchos Rellenos
Makes 1 cup.

2 cups sour cream

½ cup minced white onion

¼ cup firmly packed cilantro leaves, minced

½ teaspoon coarse sea salt

Prepare the Picadillo de Pollo. In a medium saucepan heat ¼ cup of the olive oil over medium heat and lightly fry the onion until wilted and translucent, about 4 to 5 minutes. Add garlic and cook for an additional 1 minute. Add tomatoes, thyme, and bay leaves, reduce heat to simmer, and cook for 15 minutes. Add capers, olives, and raisins and cook an additional 10 minutes, stirring often.

Meanwhile, in a heavy, 12-inch skillet or sauté pan, heat the remaining ¼ cup of the oil over high heat until smoking. Add the chicken and cook until the chicken is dry, stirring constantly. Add salt and the hot tomato sauce, reduce heat, and simmer an additional 5 minutes. Stir in the almonds and fresh herbs, remove from heat, and allow to cool.

To prepare the chiles, combine water, piloncillo, cinnamon, vinegar, and salt in a medium nonreactive saucepan. Bring to a boil, reduce heat, and simmer until piloncillo has dissolved, about 5 minutes. Add the chiles, cover, remove from heat immediately, and set aside to soak for 8 minutes. Carefully transfer the chiles one by one onto paper towels to drain.

Preheat oven to 350 degrees. Lightly grease a 13-by-9-inch baking dish. Stuff each chile with a portion of the cooled Picadillo de Pollo and arrange in the prepared baking dish. Cover with foil and bake in preheated oven for 15 to 20 minutes or until filling is heated through.

While the chiles are baking, prepare the Cream Sauce for Anchos Rellenos. Combine sour cream and onion in a 2-quart, nonreactive saucepan. Bring to a boil and boil for 8 minutes; strain. Add cilantro and salt. Keep warm.

Remove baked chiles from oven and serve immediately in a pool of warm sauce. Serves 8.

# Leonora Carrington

Untitled, date unknown. Oil, 24½ × 30½ inches.

*Leonora Carrington was born in Lancashire, England, to a wealthy family, presented to court, endured a turbulent early life—including a time when she lived with artist Max Ernst in Europe—then fled to Mexico, where she settled and focused on her work. A versatile artist throughout her long career, she painted, sculpted, and wrote short stories, plays, and novels, dedicating her life to the "love of creation."*

*T.G.*

# CHILES RELLENOS DE PICADILLO ❁
## Chiles Stuffed with Pork

This remarkable dish is served during the fall of the year when poblano chiles and pomegranates are in season. It is popular at banquets celebrating Dieciséis de Septiembre, a Mexican holiday commemorating Mexico's struggle for independence from Spain. The green chiles and red sauce are said to represent two of the three colors of the Mexican flag.

*3 pounds pork butt or shoulder, trimmed of tendons and cut into cubes*

*1 small white onion, quartered, plus 1 small white onion, chopped*

*3 whole garlic cloves plus 4 garlic cloves, chopped*

*2 teaspoons plus ½ teaspoon sea salt*

*7 tablespoons fat, skimmed from cooking broth*

*10 whole black peppercorns*

*6 whole cloves*

*1 1-inch piece of a Mexican cinnamon stick* ❁

*4 tablespoons raisins*

*3 tablespoons slivered almonds*

*3 tablespoons finely chopped candied fruit*

*4 or 5 medium tomatoes, roasted and peeled* ❁

*6 large poblano chiles, prepared for stuffing* ❁

*4 eggs, separated*

*Pinch of sea salt*

*Vegetable oil for frying*

*Flour for dredging*

*Tomato Sauce (see recipe for Huevos Motuleños)*

Put pork cubes in a stock pot and add the onion quarters, whole garlic cloves, and 2 teaspoons salt. Cover with cold water, bring to a rolling boil, lower heat, and simmer for about 45 minutes. Do not overcook. Drain the meat, reserving the cooking broth. Shred the meat with fingers or two forks and set aside. Refrigerate broth for several hours, or until the fat has risen to the top. Skim off 7 tablespoons of fat from the chilled broth; discard broth or refrigerate for another use. Heat fat in a heavy skillet over medium heat and add the chopped onion and garlic. Fry until the onion is wilted and transparent, about 5 to 7 minutes. Stir in the shredded meat and remove from heat.

In a coffee or spice grinder, grind together the peppercorns, cloves, and cinnamon stick. Add the ground spices, raisins, almonds, candied fruit, and the remaining ½ teaspoon salt to the shredded meat mixture. Mash the roasted tomatoes with a potato masher and add to the meat mixture. Cook over medium heat for about 15 minutes, or until the liquid has been absorbed. Set aside to cool. When cool enough to handle, divide into 6 equal portions, shape into ovals, and refrigerate until ready to stuff the chiles.

Stuff each of the roasted, prepared chiles with the chilled meat mixture and set aside.

In a small bowl, beat egg whites until stiff. Gently whisk in egg yolks, one at a time, and a pinch of salt. In a heavy skillet or Dutch oven, heat 1 to 2 inches of oil over medium heat. Dredge the stuffed chiles in flour and then dip them, two at a time, into the egg batter to coat. Gently slide two of the chiles into the hot oil. Fry over medium heat for 2 to 3 minutes. Using two spatulas, turn gently and cook an additional 2 to 3 minutes, or until golden brown. If necessary, use a spoon to scoop hot oil over any areas of the chiles that are not cooking completely. When the chiles are golden, remove from the hot oil with a slotted spoon and drain on paper towels. Keep in a warm oven while frying the remaining chiles. Serve hot on individual dinner plates in a pool of warm Tomato Sauce. Serves 6.

## Wine Suggestion

Vino Nobile di Montepulciano (Sangiovese)

## Variation

Replace the pork mixture with 6 cups shredded Monterey Jack cheese. Form cheese into 6 ovals, stuff the chiles, and proceed as directed. Serve with Salsa Ranchera (see recipe for Huevos Rancheros).

# CALABACITAS RELLENAS ❀
## Stuffed Zucchini Squash

This hearty vegetarian dish is Miguel's adaptation of a recipe from Diana Kennedy's seminal first cookbook, *The Cuisines of Mexico*. It has long been a favorite entrée of the restaurant's very loyal vegetarian clientele. Serve it as an entrée with a salad, Arroz Blanco, and Frijoles Refritos, or as a side dish for poultry or grilled meats.

*6 large zucchini squash*

*2 cups fresh corn kernels cut from the cob or frozen corn kernels, thawed*

*2 tablespoons milk*

*1 teaspoon sea salt*

*2 eggs*

*1 cup (4 ounces) shredded Monterey Jack cheese*

*4 tablespoons butter, softened*

*2 cups Salsa Ranchera, warmed (see recipe for Huevos Rancheros)*

Preheat oven to 350 degrees. Lightly grease a 13-by-9-inch casserole dish and set aside. Cut the zucchini in half lengthwise. Use a melon baller to scoop out the center and make small boats, discarding the pulp. (Take care not to puncture the bottom or sides of the squash.) Place in the prepared baking dish and set aside. Combine corn, milk, salt, and eggs in a blender and blend to a coarse puree. Stir in ½ cup of the shredded cheese. Divide the corn mixture into equal portions and spoon into the zucchini shells. Top each with a portion of the remaining ½ cup cheese and a dollop of butter. Cover with foil and bake for 30 to 45 minutes, or until the custard is set. Place 2 boats on each plate and spoon warm Salsa Ranchera over the top. Serves 6 as an entrée or 12 as a side dish.

# ENCHILADAS SAN MIGUEL

Enchiladas are tortillas that are glazed in a small amount of hot fat to soften them, then dipped in sauce, filled with meat, cheese, or vegetables, rolled up, and swathed in additional sauce. They are a staple of the Mexican diet and vary from house to house and cook to cook. Miguel offers enchiladas with pork, chicken, cheese, or crabmeat fillings and a choice of sauces: Mole Poblano, Salsa Verde, or Sour Cream Sauce. The side dishes are Arroz Mexicano and Frijoles Refritos. Enchiladas aren't difficult to make per se, but getting all the components prepared dictates some work before the final assembly can begin. For the best-tasting results, make the fillings and sauces well ahead of time and reheat just in time to assemble the final product when it's time to eat. Share the fun by having an assembly line to put the enchiladas together.

> *Your choice of sauce, such as Mole Poblano, Salsa Verde for Enchiladas, or*
>   *Sour Cream Sauce*
>
> *Pork Filling or Chicken Filling (see below), or substitute your choice of filling*
>
> *6 tablespoons vegetable oil*
>
> *12 corn tortillas*

Prepare your choice of sauce and keep warm; or reheat when ready to assemble enchiladas. Prepare the Pork Filling or Chicken Filling and keep hot or reheat.

  In a small skillet, heat oil over medium-high heat until it shimmers. (Make sure the oil is hot enough, or the tortillas will absorb too much oil and be greasy.) Using tongs, dip each tortilla into the hot oil for about 10 to 15 seconds, or until softened. Drain on paper towels. Working quickly, dip each tortilla in the warm sauce. Lay each tortilla flat, put 3 to 4 tablespoons of hot filling down the center of the tortilla, and roll it into a tube. Serve 2 enchiladas per plate and cover with warm sauce. Serve immediately or the enchiladas will get soggy. Serves 6.

## Pork Filling

Makes 3 cups (fills 12 enchiladas).

> *2 pounds pork butt or shoulder, trimmed of tendons and cut into 1-inch cubes*
>
> *1 teaspoon sea salt*
>
> *1 pound Mexican chorizo, casings removed*
>
> *6 medium tomatoes, peeled and chopped* ✽
>
> *1 medium white onion, chopped*
>
> *½ teaspoon dried Mexican oregano*
>
> *½ teaspoon dried thyme*
>
> *3 bay leaves*
>
> *6 chipotle chiles in adobo sauce, chopped* ✽
>
> *5 tablespoons adobo sauce from the can*
>
> *¾ cup broth, reserved from cooking pork*

Put meat in a stock pot, cover with cold water, add salt, and bring to a boil over medium heat. Reduce heat to low and simmer for 30 or 45 minutes, or until meat is tender. Drain the meat, reserving the broth. When the meat is cool enough to handle, shred with your fingers or two forks and set aside. In a heavy, 14-inch skillet or Dutch oven, fry the chorizo over medium-high heat. Skim off some of the grease if the amount seems unappealing, but leave enough to cook the remaining ingredients. Increase heat to high, add the tomatoes and onion, and cook for 3 to 5 minutes, stirring often. Add the shredded pork, oregano, thyme, bay leaves, chiles, adobo sauce, and ¾ cup of the reserved broth. Stir to blend well. Reduce heat to medium and cook for about 15 minutes, stirring often. Keep warm or reheat before filling enchiladas.

## Chicken Filling

Makes 3 cups (fills 12 enchiladas).

> *6 ounces Mexican chorizo, casings removed*
>
> *¼ cup chopped white onion*
>
> *2 garlic cloves, chopped*
>
> *4 medium tomatoes, roasted and chopped* ✿
>
> *3 chipotle chiles in adobo sauce* ✿
>
> *2 tablespoons adobo sauce from the can*
>
> *2 to 3 boneless chicken breasts, poached in water seasoned with sea salt and ground black pepper, then cooled and shredded (about 2 cups)*
>
> *⅓ cup chicken broth, reserved from cooking chicken*
>
> *Sea salt and ground black pepper to taste*

Crumble chorizo into a heavy, 12-inch skillet or Dutch oven. Cook over low heat to render the fat, but do not allow it to brown. Strain off fat, returning 3 tablespoons of fat to the skillet. Add the onion and garlic and cook over low heat, stirring constantly until onions are wilted and transparent. Add tomatoes, chiles, and adobo sauce. Increase heat to medium and cook, stirring often, until all moisture has been absorbed and the mixture is dry, about 15 minutes. Stir in shredded chicken and broth. Cook another 3 to 4 minutes, until chicken is heated through. Season to taste with salt and pepper.

*NOTE:* The pork and chicken enchilada fillings can also be used as fillings for tacos and quesadillas as well as toppings for tostadas or *sopes*.

## Wine Suggestion

Petite Syrah (with Mole Poblano), Sancerre (with Salsa Verde)

# ENCHILADAS SUIZAS DE JAIBA
## Crabmeat Enchiladas with Sour Cream Sauce

The flavorful crabmeat mixture used as a filling for these distinctive enchiladas comes from the Caribbean coast of Mexico. So that the delicate flavor of the crab isn't overwhelmed by a strong sauce, Miguel serves them with the creamy Sour Cream Sauce, as pictured, or a mixture of Salsa Verde and Sour Cream Sauce. The filling in this recipe can also be used for quesadillas or as a topping for *sopes*.

*6 tablespoons vegetable oil*
*12 corn tortillas*
*Crabmeat Filling (see below)*
*Sour Cream Sauce (see below)*

### Crabmeat Filling

Makes 3 cups (fills 12 enchiladas).

*1¼ pounds lump crabmeat*
*6 tablespoons olive oil*
*3 tablespoons butter*
*3 garlic cloves, chopped*
*1 medium white onion, chopped*
*2 pickled jalapeños, chopped, with ¼ cup liquid from the can* ✽
*2 or 3 pickled carrots, chopped*
*2 medium tomatoes, seeded and chopped*
*¼ cup chopped fresh parsley*
*¼ cup chopped fresh cilantro*
*Sea salt and ground black pepper to taste*

### Sour Cream Sauce

Makes 3¾ cups.

*3 cups sour cream*
*¾ cup milk*
*1 teaspoon sea salt*
*1 teaspoon ground white pepper*

Prepare the Crabmeat Filling. Pick through the crabmeat and remove any bits of shell or cartilage, taking care not to break up the lumps. In a heavy nonreactive skillet, heat the oil and butter over medium heat, add garlic and onion, and sauté until the onion is wilted and transparent. Add the jalapeños and juice, carrots, tomatoes, parsley, and cilantro and cook for about 3 minutes; season to taste with salt and pepper. Reduce heat to low and cook until mixture thickens, about 20 minutes. Add crabmeat and cook just until crabmeat is heated through. Adjust seasonings as needed. Keep warm.

Prepare the Sour Cream Sauce. Whisk the ingredients together in a small bowl and set aside.

In a small skillet, heat oil over medium-high heat. Soften the tortillas in the oil, following the procedure described in the recipe for Enchiladas San Miguel. Place 3 tablespoons Crabmeat Filling down the center of each tortilla and roll it up. Arrange the enchiladas on an ovenproof serving platter or baking dish. Top with Sour Cream Sauce, place under a broiler for 3 minutes, and serve immediately. Serves 6 to 8.

### Wine Suggestion

Australian Riesling

### Variation

Stir together 1 recipe Salsa Verde for Enchiladas and 1 recipe Sour Cream Sauce. After softening tortillas in oil, dip in the warm sauce mixture and fill with Crabmeat Filling as directed. Cover with a generous serving of the sauce mixture.

# ENCHILADAS SUIZAS DE QUESO
## Cheese Enchiladas with Sour Cream Sauce

These "Swiss" enchiladas are a famous Mexico City dish, reputed to have been created at the lunch counter restaurant in the renowned Sanborn's department store. Traditionally they are filled with chicken or cheese and served in individual oval baking dishes. The enchiladas are then topped with tangy Salsa Verde and slathered with Sour Cream Sauce. Put the plates under the broiler for 30 seconds to 1 minute to make sure the sauces are bubbling hot.

*1½ cup shredded Monterey Jack cheese*
*½ cup diced white onion*
*6 tablespoons vegetable oil*
*12 corn tortillas*
*Sour Cream Sauce (see recipe for Enchiladas Suizas de Jaiba)*

### Salsa Verde for Enchiladas
Makes 2 cups.

*15 tomatillos, husked* ❋
*Half of a medium white onion*
*1 garlic clove*
*4 to 6 serrano chiles* ❋
*¼ cup chopped cilantro leaves*
*Sea salt to taste*

Prepare the Salsa Verde for Enchiladas. Roast tomatillos, onion, garlic, and chiles on a comal or griddle until they are blistered all over. Combine the roasted vegetables in a food processor and process until smooth. When ready to serve, add cilantro. Adjust seasonings, adding salt if necessary. Set aside.

Preheat broiler and place oven rack 3 inches below heat source. Combine the shredded cheese and onion in a bowl, tossing to blend well. In a small skillet, heat oil over medium-high heat. Soften the tortillas in the oil, following the procedure described in the recipe for Enchiladas San Miguel. Dip each softened tortilla in the Salsa Verde for Enchiladas.

Place 3 tablespoons of the cheese mixture down the center of each tortilla and roll it up. Arrange 2 enchiladas on each serving plate. Top with additional Salsa Verde and a generous dollop of Sour Cream Sauce. Run each plate under the preheated broiler for about 30 seconds to 1 minute, or until the cheese filling is melted and the sour cream is bubbling. Serve immediately. Serves 6.

### Wine Suggestion
German Riesling

## Juan Vicente Rodríguez Bonachea

*Tucán*, 1992. Oil, 31 × 39 inches.

*Rodríguez Bonachea captured other worlds full of magic. I was entranced when I found this painting in Merida, Mexico, and I purchased it on the spot. Rodríguez Bonachea was also a book illustrator, engraver, and teacher, and he exhibited around the world. He was only fifty-five when he died of a stroke in 2012.*

T.G.

# TAMALES WITH SHRIMP AND SCALLOP CREAM SAUCE

My cousin, Steven Ravago, who is a chef in San Diego, California, gave me this idea.

## Tamales

*15 ounces unsalted butter*

*9 tablespoons sour cream*

*3 tablespoons paprika (optional)*

*2 teaspoons salt, or to taste*

*½ teaspoon baking powder*

*1 pound freshly made white corn masa (dough)*

*2½ cups chicken broth (if needed)*

*40 dried corn husks (soaked), 2 per tamale*

Using a mixer, beat the softened butter for 5 minutes to aerate it. Add sour cream, paprika (optional), salt, baking powder, and masa. Add chicken broth as needed until the mixture is a thick, moist batter. Overlap two corn husks lengthwise and spread masa over their width and to about 1 inch from either end. Fold in thirds and tie at both ends. You can tear ⅛-inch thick lengthwise strips of soaked corn husks to use for ties. Place vertically in a steamer and cook for approximately 45 to 55 minutes.

## Chile Paste

*9 whole ancho chiles, stemmed and seeded*

*3 tablespoons rice vinegar*

*9 cloves garlic*

*1½ teaspoons dried Mexican oregano*

*¾ teaspoon salt*

Place chiles in a bowl, cover with boiling water, and allow to soak for 30 minutes. Drain and transfer chiles to a blender. Add the vinegar, garlic, oregano, and salt. Blend until smooth and set aside. You should have about 12 tablespoons of paste.

## Shrimp and Scallop Sauce

*9 tablespoons butter or olive oil*

*40 whole medium-size shrimp, peeled and deveined (leave tails on)*

*20 whole sea scallops, cleaned*

*¾ cup tequila*

*4½ cups heavy cream*

*Salt and pepper to taste*

*Chopped flat-leaf parsley for garnish*

Heat butter or olive oil in a large skillet over medium heat. Add the shrimp and scallops. Sauté until the shrimp turns pink and the scallops are done, approximately 3 to 5 minutes. Remove skillet from heat, add tequila, and ignite with a long lighter. Be careful and stand back, because the flames can be quite spectacular. Return skillet to heat and cook, stirring with caution, until the flames subside. Using a slotted spoon, remove shrimp and scallops to a bowl. Cover with foil to keep warm. Cook the remaining tequila over medium-high heat for another minute to reduce. Add the chile paste and simmer for another 7 minutes. Then lower heat, add heavy cream to skillet, and simmer until reduced to a sauce consistency, about 5 minutes. Add salt and pepper to taste.

Place four shrimp and a scallop, along with a spoonful of the chile cream, on each tamale before serving. Garnish with parsley. Serves 10.

# CARNE ASADA A LA TAMPIQUEÑA ✣
## Grilled Steak, Tampico Style

This grilled tenderloin, cut in a special way, is a signature dish from the Mexican coastal city of Tampico. Traditionally the strip of steak is served with Rajas y Cebollas, a cheese enchilada, Frijoles Refritos, and Guacamole. Fonda San Miguel purchases the excellent beef tenderloin for this dish from Niman Ranch in California. The tenderloin is sliced into a very thin rectangular strip, no more than ¼-inch thick, using a series of butterfly cuts. For best results, purchase a piece of meat that the butcher has cut from the center of the tenderloin (such as the chateaubriand cut) and then chill the meat before slicing it. To slice the meat as thin as possible, Miguel uses a serrated knife with a broad, flexible blade.

*1 pound piece of beef tenderloin, trimmed, with silverskin removed*
*1 teaspoon vegetable oil*
*Sea salt and ground black pepper to taste*

Lay the piece of tenderloin on a cutting board. Pressing down on the meat with the palm of the hand, position the cutting edge of the knife against one side of the tenderloin, with the surface of the blade parallel to the cutting board. The distance between the knife and the cutting board should be about ¼ inch. Carefully slice the meat with a horizontal motion, keeping the blade straight and level so the thickness of the slice will be uniform. Continue slicing until the leading edge of the knife is within 1 inch of the other side of the tenderloin (make sure that you don't slice all the way through). Grasp the thick part of the meat and turn it over, sliced side facing down and lying flat on the cutting board. Position the knife directly above where the sliced strip is connected to the thick part of the meat, with the blade touching the sliced strip. Using the same technique and keeping the knife blade about ¼ inch above the surface of the cutting board, again slice the meat to within 1 inch of the other side and turn it over. Work carefully so the sliced strip stays in one piece and is a uniform thickness of ¼ inch. (Thicker areas can be pressed or pounded to get a more even thickness.) Continue this process as though you were unfolding the meat into a long, narrow rectangle measuring about 10 to 12 inches in length (the width will depend on the size of the section cut from the tenderloin to yield the required weight). Slice the finished strip in half crosswise to make two steaks about 5 or 6 inches long. For easier handling, you can roll up the strips like jelly rolls until you are ready to grill them.

Preheat gas grill to 350 degrees or medium-hot. Rub the meat pieces with oil and season to taste with salt and pepper. Sear the meat for 1 minute on each side for medium-rare. (Watch it closely; it will cook quickly because it is so thin.) Serves 2.

## Wine Suggestion
California Zinfandel

# TAMALES CON RAJAS Y CEBOLLAS

## Tamales with Strips of Roasted Poblano Chiles and Onions

The masa for these tamales is rich in flavor but light in texture and is perfect for a variety of fillings. Miguel uses the tamales stuffed with poblano *rajas* and grilled onions as a side dish with different meats, but they can just as easily be served as a meatless entrée. Good vegetarian filling alternatives would be Frijoles Refritos and panela cheese or sautéed mushrooms in adobo sauce.

*⅔ cup butter, softened*

*1¼ cups sour cream*

*1 tablespoon sea salt*

*6 cups masa harina, reconstituted according to directions on the package*

*2 tablespoons baking powder*

*5 teaspoons chili powder*

*30 corn husks* ✿

*1 recipe Rajas y Cebollas (see separate recipe)*

In the mixing bowl of a stand mixer with a paddle attachment, beat the butter 4 to 5 minutes, or until fluffy. Add sour cream, salt, masa, baking powder, and chili powder; beat until well blended. Cover dough and allow to rest for 15 minutes.

While dough is resting, cover the corn husks with boiling water and allow to soak for 15 to 20 minutes, or until pliable. Drain and pat dry.

Spoon 1 heaping tablespoon of dough down the middle of a corn husk, spread dough to form a 3-inch square. Put 1 to 2 tablespoons Rajas y Cebollas in the center of the square. Fold one half of the corn husk over the filling and fold the other half to cover. Fold up the bottom (tapered) flap to seal one end. Repeat with the remaining corn husks.

In a tamale steamer or stock pot with a metal rack, pour in enough water to reach the rack. Stand the tamales close together on the rack, open ends facing up. Cover with a damp cloth and foil or the pot lid. Bring the water to a simmer over medium heat and steam tamales for 30 to 45 minutes, checking often to make sure the steamer does not boil dry. Serves 6 to 8.

# RAJAS Y CEBOLLAS
## Strips of Roasted Poblano Chiles and Onions

These strips of roasted poblano chiles and onions are a very functional side dish or condiment for grilled meats and many other dishes. They are also an important component of Carne Asada a la Tampiqueña, a great garnish for all kinds of tacos, and a simple and delicious filling for tamales.

*2 tablespoons olive oil*

*4 poblano chiles, roasted, peeled, seeded, and sliced lengthwise into ¼-inch strips* ❋

*1 medium white onion, cut into ¼-inch slices*

*1 teaspoon coarse sea salt*

In a medium skillet, heat oil over medium heat. Add chiles and onions and cook for 5 to 7 minutes, or until onions are wilted and transparent. Sprinkle with salt and serve hot or at room temperature. Serves 6 to 8 as a condiment.

### Iker Larrauri

*Toro rojo*, 1994.
Oil on canvas,
65 × 97 inches.

*Fonda San Miguel is quite fortunate to have two very large canvases by Iker Larrauri, who happens to be the stepfather of one of our former chefs, Roberto Santibáñez. The first one I purchased was the one of the red bull, in which the bull appears to be flying over a Mad Max–like scene in Mexico City a hundred years from now. Then I wanted a companion piece, so I asked Roberto's stepfather if he would paint another large work so they could be hung together. He came up with a blue horse to go with the red bull. Sometimes we hang the paintings together; sometimes we display one and put the other in storage. No matter which one is up, people ask about the other: "Where's the big red bull?" "What happened to the blue horse?" Iker Larrauri is a painter, sculptor, and muralist who painted the big murals in the Museo Nacional de Antropología in Mexico City. When you walk around the first floor of this renowned museum, you see Iker's monumental murals.*

*T.G.*

# AGUJAS DE RES
## Beef Short Ribs, Yucatan Style

This is one of Miguel's favorite barbecue dishes from the Yucatan, and it utilizes the same Achiote Rub as Cochinita Pibil. The recipe is traditionally made with beef ribs, but when the restaurant began purchasing pork from Niman Ranch, Miguel experimented with the St. Louis pork ribs and customers went wild. Now, when the pork ribs run as a nightly special, they sell out as quickly as the beef. Whether using pork or beef, Miguel serves this dish with Frijoles Negros and Ensalada de Tres Chiles. The dish takes two days to make, but it is well worth the investment.

> *4½ pounds beef short ribs, cut into 16 pieces*
> *Achiote Rub (see recipe for Cochinita Pibil)*
> *2 to 4 banana leaves ✽*
> *½ cup cold water*
> *Fresh tortillas, heated on a comal*
> *Salsa of your choice*

Rub the ribs with the Achiote Rub and set aside. Using tongs, carefully sear each banana leaf over an open flame until flexible. Divide the ribs into equal portions and wrap each portion in a banana leaf. Put in a large nonreactive dish, cover, and refrigerate for 24 hours.

Preheat oven to 350 degrees. Place a rack in the bottom of a heavy Dutch oven and set the wrapped meat on the rack. Add cold water and cover with a tight-fitting lid. Cook for 2½ hours, turn the wrapped meat, and baste the outside of the banana leaves with the juices from the bottom of the pot. Cook another 30 to 45 minutes, remove from oven, and carefully unwrap meat to check it. The meat should fall off the bone. Transfer the meat to 8 warm dinner plates and serve with fresh tortillas and salsa so that guests can make their own tacos. Serves 8.

## Variation

Substitute thick-cut pork ribs for the beef and follow the recipe as directed.

Iker Larrauri

*Caballo azul,* 1999.
Oil on canvas,
65 × 97 inches.

# MIXIOTE WITH LAMB SHANKS

Serving-size packages of meat seasoned with chile and other spices, then steamed.

*7 pasilla chiles*

*8 guajillo chiles, roasted, seeded, and deveined*

*1 bottle dark Mexican beer*

*8 cloves garlic, peeled*

*½ white onion, chopped*

*¼ teaspoon cumin seeds, toasted (be careful not to scorch or burn)*

*½ teaspoon dried Mexican oregano*

*¼ teaspoon marjoram*

*¼ teaspoon dried thyme*

*6 lamb shanks*

*1 jar nopales for topping meat in the packages (optional)*

*Salt to taste*

## Chile Paste

Soak the chiles in warm water for 15 minutes.

In a blender, puree the soaked and drained chiles, adding the beer a little at a time. Add garlic, onion, cumin, oregano, marjoram, and thyme. Blend together until smooth. You can do this step in batches if necessary.

Coat each lamb shank with chile paste and, for best results, cover and refrigerate overnight.

Place each lamb shank on a 12-inch square of parchment paper, and top with 1 tablespoon nopales (optional). Make a sealed "package" of each. Place packages in the top part of a steamer and add the rest of the beer with chile (or water) to the bottom of the steamer. Place a coin in the bottom of the steamer; it will rattle if the water is running low. Be sure there is enough water to continuously steam the packages.

Bring the water to a boil and cook the packages until the meat is fork-tender. This could take 2½ to 3 hours. Each package should have plenty of juice.

Serve in deep bowls, like pasta bowls, with hot corn or flour tortillas. Serves 6.

# ELOTES

## Corn on the Cob with Crab Butter

Butter and seafood are two of sweet corn's classic partners. In this recipe, all three are wrapped together with spice and a punch to the palate.

*¼ pound (1 stick) unsalted butter, room temperature*

*Zest of ½ lemon plus a squeeze of juice*

*½ teaspoon cayenne pepper*

*¾ teaspoon ground mace (or substitute ground nutmeg)*

*¼ teaspoon salt*

*Freshly ground black pepper to taste*

*3½ pounds mixed brown and white crabmeat, cleaned*

*8 ears corn on the cob*

*1 tablespoon olive oil for griddling*

*¼ cup chopped chives*

In a medium bowl, beat together the butter, lemon zest, lemon juice, spices, salt, and freshly ground black pepper. Fold in the crabmeat until well combined. Transfer the mixture to a large sheet of parchment paper and shape until it roughly resembles a sausage. Chill for 30 minutes or until firm.

Heat a griddle until hot. Rub the corn ears lightly with olive oil and cook for 2 to 3 minutes on each side or until tender and slightly charred. This process will take a total of approximately 12 to 15 minutes.

For serving, plate the hot ears of corn and top them with slices of the crab butter. Sprinkle with chopped chives and serve. Serves 8.

# COCHINITA PIBIL ✽
## Pork Cooked in a Pit

Cochinita Pibil is the traditional pork barbecue of the Yucatan Peninsula, where for centuries it has been cooked in pits lined with hot stones and banana leaves. The achiote-based rub, which imparts a rich, terra-cotta color and an earthy flavor, is equally good on seafood and chicken.

*4 pounds pork shoulder or butt, trimmed of tendons and cut into 1-inch cubes*

*2 tablespoons safflower oil*

*4 large tomatoes, sliced*

*2 medium white onions, sliced*

*2 tablespoons reserved Achiote Rub (see below)*

*1 large banana leaf* ✽

*Cebollas Rojas en Escabeche (see separate recipe)*

*Arroz Blanco* ✤

### Achiote Rub

*2 tablespoons achiote seeds or 3 tablespoons achiote paste* ✽

*¼ cup orange juice*

*¼ cup distilled white vinegar*

*½ teaspoon cumin seeds*

*½ teaspoon dried Mexican oregano*

*12 whole black peppercorns*

*4 whole allspice*

*8 garlic cloves, peeled*

*¼ teaspoon paprika*

*1 tablespoon sea salt*

Prepare the Achiote Rub. Mix the achiote seeds with the orange juice and vinegar and soak 1 hour to soften them. Using a *molcajete* or mortar and pestle, crush the achiote seeds with a little of the soaking liquid. Transfer the seeds and soaking liquid to a blender and add the remaining rub ingredients; blend to a paste. Reserve 2 tablespoons of the paste for cooking with the tomatoes. Rub the pork cubes with the Achiote Rub and set aside.

Heat oil in a heavy skillet over medium heat. Add tomatoes, onions, and the reserved 2 tablespoons of Achiote Rub. Fry for about 3 minutes and set aside.

Preheat oven to 350 degrees. Have a large, heavy Dutch oven ready. Using tongs, carefully sear the banana leaf over an open flame until flexible. Line the Dutch oven with the banana leaf and arrange the pork cubes on the leaf. Cover the pork with the tomato mixture, folding the banana leaf over the top. Cover and cook in preheated oven for 2 to 2½ hours, basting occasionally with juices from the bottom of the pot. Remove from the oven and transfer to a serving platter. Garnish with Cebollas Rojas en Escabeche and serve with Arroz Blanco. Serves 6.

*NOTE*: If using prepared achiote paste instead of achiote seeds, skip the soaking and crushing step. Simply mash the paste with the orange juice and vinegar and then transfer the mixture to a blender.

### Wine Suggestion

Burgundian Pinot Noir

### Variation

Substitute 4 pounds chicken pieces for the pork. Brown in a skillet with a little oil. Proceed as directed.

# BORREGO
## Lamb Loin Chops in Chipotle Rub

An ardent supporter of the Slow Food movement, Tom is a stickler for serving customers only the best-quality ingredients available. The meat for these delicious lamb chops comes from Jamison Farms in Latrobe, Pennsylvania. The lamb is grass-fed as well as hormone, pesticide, and antibiotic free. Miguel serves this dish with Chipotle Potato Gratin and a mixed green salad. The spicy salt rub is good for lamb chops, pork chops, or steak, and it is also great on corn on the cob! Any unused rub can be stored at room temperature in a sealed container and reground before using it again.

*24 2½-ounce loin lamb chops*
*Olive oil to coat*

### Chipotle Rub

*¼ cup corn oil*

*7 dried chipotle chiles, seeds and veins removed* ✽

*2 ancho chiles, seeds and veins removed* ✽

*12 garlic cloves, peeled*

*¾ cup coarse sea salt*

*¼ cup dried Mexican oregano, toasted*

Prepare the Chipotle Rub. Heat corn oil in a heavy skillet over medium-high heat until hot but not smoking. Fry the chiles, 1 or 2 at a time, turning once, until they puff up and brown, about 10 to 15 seconds each. Do not allow them to burn, or the rub will be bitter. Remove with a slotted spoon and drain on paper towels. Set aside until chiles are cool and crisp. (You can either discard the oil or save it in a jar to flavor soups, stews, and sauces.) Once the chiles have cooled, grind them in batches in a spice grinder until they are a fine powder. Combine the ground chiles, garlic, salt, and toasted oregano in a food processor and process until the mixture is coarse and salt-like. If the rub seems wet, spread it in an even layer on a baking sheet and allow it to dry in a cool (150-degree) oven until it is no longer moist, about 1 hour. Break up any lumps with your fingers.

Preheat a gas grill to 350 degrees. Rub the meat with olive oil and a generous portion of the Chipotle Rub. Place chops on the grill and cook for 2 to 3 minutes, or until browned on one side. Turn and cook an additional 2 to 3 minutes for medium. Serves 6.

### Wine Suggestion
Argentinean Mapoundec

### Variation
Substitute 1½-inch-thick pork chops and proceed as directed.

### Wine Suggestion
Cru Beaujolais from Moulin-à-Vent (Gamay)

# PARRILLADA DE LA FRONTERA NORTEÑA
## Mixed Grill from the Border

This platter of grilled and fried meats is a very popular dish along the border between the northern states of Mexico and the southwestern United States—*la frontera norteña*. All the meats are grilled except the frog legs, which are dredged in seasoned flour and fried. A good-quality butcher shop can help you locate the necessary game meats and sweetbreads and will remove the membranes from the sweetbreads, if you ask. Both quail and frog legs are available frozen these days. The grilled meats can simply be seasoned with salt and pepper, but the Chipotle Rub is also a good choice here. Serve the meats on a sizzling platter with a side of Salsa Mexicana, Ensalada de Nopalitos, and plenty of warm flour or corn tortillas.

*4 ounces venison tenderloin*

*5 ounces sweetbreads, cut in half lengthwise*

*1 semi-boneless quail*

*2 tablespoons vegetable oil*

*Sea salt and ground black pepper to taste, or substitute Chipotle Rub (see recipe for Borrego)*

*1 pair frog legs*

*½ cup all-purpose flour, seasoned with 1 teaspoon sea salt and ½ teaspoon chili powder*

*Vegetable oil for frying*

Preheat gas grill to 350 degrees. Rub venison, sweetbreads, and quail with the oil. Season with salt and pepper. Dredge frog legs in the seasoned flour and shake off excess. Set aside.

Grill quail 4 to 5 minutes, turn, and cook an additional 4 to 5 minutes. Grill venison 4 minutes, turn, and cook an additional 3 minutes. Grill sweetbreads 1 minute, turn, cook an additional 1 minute, turn again, and cook an additional 1 minute on the first side.

While the meat is grilling, heat 1 to 2 inches of oil in a heavy skillet over medium-high heat until it shimmers. Fry frog legs 2 minutes on each side. Drain on paper towels. Serve grilled meats and fried frog legs on a sizzling platter. Serves 1.

## Wine Suggestion
Rioja Gran Reserva (Tempranillo)

# PIPIÁN VERDE
## Game Hen in Ground Nut Sauce with Tomatillos

Classic *pipianes* are sauces thickened with ground nuts and seeds and flavored with herbs and spices. The hearty sauce used in this dish comes from central Mexico, where it is served with roast duckling, pork, and chicken. Miguel often serves it as a special over Cornish game hens, accompanied by Arroz Blanco and Frijoles Negros.

> *6 small Cornish game hens*
> *Olive oil*
> *Sea salt and ground black pepper to taste*

## Ground Nut Sauce with Tomatillos ✿
Makes about 5¼ cups.

> *18 to 20 tomatillos, husked and rinsed (about 1 pound)* ✽
> *4 serrano chiles (or fewer for a milder dish)* ✽
> *⅓ cup dry-roasted peanuts*
> *½ cup pumpkin seeds, toasted* ✽
> *Half of a medium white onion, chopped*
> *3 garlic cloves, chopped*
> *½ cup chopped cilantro leaves*
> *1 sprig fresh epazote, chopped* ✽
> *1 teaspoon sea salt*
> *4 cups reserved cooking water*
> *2 tablespoons vegetable oil*

Preheat oven to 350 degrees. Rub the game hens inside and out with olive oil, salt, and pepper. Place hens, not touching, in a large open roasting pan and roast for 30 to 45 minutes. Test for doneness by inserting a knife into the leg joint. When juices run clear, the hens are done.

While the hens are cooking, prepare the Ground Nut Sauce with Tomatillos. Put the tomatillos in a heavy, 4-quart saucepan and add water to cover. Bring to a boil over medium heat. Lower heat to a brisk simmer; cook until soft. Drain tomatillos, reserving the cooking water. Combine tomatillos, chiles, peanuts, pumpkin seeds, onion, garlic, fresh herbs, and salt in a blender and process until smooth, using the reserved cooking water and additional water as needed, up to 4 cups. In a heavy nonreactive Dutch oven or skillet, heat vegetable oil over medium heat and add the tomatillo mixture. Cook for about 20 minutes, stirring often so it does not stick.

Ladle a small pool of the Ground Nut Sauce with Tomatillos on each plate; place a hen in the center of the sauce and top with an additional generous serving of sauce. Serves 6.

## Wine Suggestion
New Zealand Sauvignon Blanc

# POLLO ASADO
## Grilled Chicken

The fajita craze that has spread across the Southwest in the last few decades inspired many restaurants to serve not only grilled beef but grilled chicken, shrimp, or vegetables and to call them "fajitas." This is actually a misnomer, because the term *fajita* refers to a specific cut of beef—skirt steak. Regardless of what you call it, this fajita-like dish of marinated, grilled chicken is delicious. The grilled chicken strips should be wrapped in flour tortillas and garnished with the same condiments served with a beef fajita platter—guacamole, cheese, Salsa Mexicana, and sour cream.

*4 pounds boneless, skinless chicken breasts or chicken tenders*

*3 tablespoons vegetable oil*

*2 poblano chiles, roasted, peeled, seeded, and sliced* ✽

*2 large red bell peppers, thinly sliced*

*2 small white onions, thinly sliced*

*Fresh flour tortillas, warmed*

*Guacamole*

*Sour cream*

*Shredded Monterey Jack cheese*

*Salsa Mexicana* ❖

### Grilled Chicken Marinade

*¼ cup freshly squeezed lime juice*

*¼ cup Worcestershire sauce*

*2 tablespoons soy sauce*

*½ teaspoon ground black pepper*

*Half of a medium white onion, sliced*

*4 garlic cloves, chopped*

Preheat gas grill to 350 degrees. Combine marinade ingredients in a nonreactive bowl. Dip the chicken pieces into the marinade just before putting them on the preheated grill. Cook 4 minutes on each side for breasts, 2½ to 3 minutes for tenders. When the juices run clear, the meat is done.

While the chicken is grilling, heat the oil in a heavy skillet over medium-high heat. Sauté chiles, bell peppers, and onions just until the onions begin to brown, about 10 to 12 minutes. Remove from heat.

To serve, slice the grilled chicken meat in strips on the diagonal and arrange on a platter. Top with the sautéed peppers and onions. Serve with fresh tortillas, guacamole, sour cream, shredded Monterey Jack cheese, and Salsa Mexicana. Serves 6 to 8.

### Wine Suggestion

Austrian Grüner Veltliner

# POLLO EN MOLE POBLANO ❁
## Chicken in Mole, Puebla Style

If there is one dish that could be considered Mexican haute cuisine, then Mole Poblano is surely it. Legend has it that the voluptuous sauce—a blend of chiles, spices, and chocolate—was created by the European Catholic nuns of Puebla to honor a visiting bishop. There are no shortcuts to making a true Mole Poblano: it takes time and patience to develop the layers of flavor that make this sauce fit for royalty. Miguel adapted the restaurant's recipe from one he learned from Diana Kennedy. At Fonda San Miguel, this mole is served with chicken and rice and as a sauce for enchiladas. It is also wonderful on roast turkey and pork.

*4 pounds chicken pieces, skin on*

*Sea salt and ground black pepper to taste*

*2 tablespoons sesame seeds, toasted, for garnish*

*Arroz Blanco* ❖

### Mole Poblano

Makes 9 cups.

*9 mulato chiles* ✽

*7 pasilla chiles* ✽

*6 ancho chiles* ✽

*1 cup plus 9 tablespoons vegetable oil or lard plus additional as needed*

*4 or 5 tomatillos, husked and cooked until soft* ✽

*5 whole cloves*

*20 whole black peppercorns*

*1-inch piece of a Mexican cinnamon stick* ✽

*1 tablespoon seeds from the chiles, toasted*

*½ teaspoon anise seeds, toasted*

*¼ teaspoon coriander seeds, toasted*

*8 tablespoons sesame seeds, toasted*

*4 garlic cloves, roasted*

*3 tablespoons raisins*

*20 whole almonds, blanched*

*¼ cup pumpkin seeds* ✽

*2 corn tortillas, torn into pieces*

*3 stale French rolls, cut into 1-inch slices*

*6 to 7 cups reserved chicken broth as needed*

*1½ ounces Mexican chocolate, chopped* ✽

In a large stock pot, parboil the chicken in water seasoned with salt and pepper to taste. Drain, reserving cooking broth, and refrigerate until ready to assemble the dish.

Prepare the Mole Poblano. Clean the chiles by removing stems, veins, and seeds; reserve 1 tablespoon of the seeds. Heat ½ cup of the oil in a heavy skillet until it shimmers. Fry the chiles until crisp, about 10 to 15 seconds, turning once; make sure they do not burn. Drain on paper towels. Put the chiles in a nonreactive bowl, cover with hot water, and set aside for 30 minutes. Drain the chiles, reserving the soaking water. Puree the chiles in a blender with enough of the soaking water to make a smooth paste. It may be necessary to scrape down the sides and blend several times to obtain a smooth paste. In a heavy Dutch oven heat an additional ½ cup oil over medium heat and add the chile puree (be careful—it will splatter). Cook for about 15 minutes, stirring often. Remove from heat and set aside.

Puree the tomatillos in a blender. In a coffee or spice grinder, grind the cloves, peppercorns, cinnamon, and toasted seeds. Add the seed mixture and the garlic to the pureed tomatillos and blend until smooth. Set aside.

Heat 6 tablespoons of the oil in a heavy frying pan. Fry each of the following ingredients and then remove with a slotted spoon: the raisins until they puff up; the almonds to a golden brown; the pumpkin seeds until they pop. If necessary, add enough oil to make 4 tablespoons and fry the tortilla pieces and bread slices until golden brown, about 15 seconds per side; remove from the skillet with a slotted spoon. Add raisins, almonds, pumpkin seeds, tortillas, and bread to the tomatillo puree and blend, using 1 to 2 cups of the reserved chicken broth, as needed, to make a smooth sauce. This may have to be done in batches. In a heavy Dutch oven, heat 3 tablespoons of the

*(Continued on next page)*

oil over medium heat. Add the chile puree, the tomatillo puree, and the Mexican chocolate (be careful—it will splatter). Cook over medium heat for about 15 minutes, stirring often. Add the remaining 5 cups of chicken broth, and cook over low heat for an additional 45 minutes, stirring often enough to prevent the mixture from scorching on the bottom. During the last 15 minutes of cooking time, add the parboiled chicken and heat through. Garnish with toasted sesame seeds and serve with Arroz Blanco. Serves 8.

*NOTE:* For easier serving, chunks of boneless, skinless chicken can be used.

## Wine Suggestion

Alsace Gewürztraminer

# POLLO EN MOLE DE ZARZAMORAS
## Chicken in Blackberry Mole

There are many classic mole recipes from the different states of Mexico, but this is a true original. Mexico City native Roberto Santibáñez was chef at Fonda San Miguel from late 1998 until early 2001, and this mole was one of his most popular signature dishes. He had never even written it down, much less published it, until he agreed to share it for this book. Roberto created this exotic mole in Mexico City with his sister around 1990 for the opening of their first restaurant, La Circunstancia, and then later brought it with him to Fonda San Miguel. The recipe is easy to prepare, and no *metate* is required—only a single 6- or 7-inch frying pan and a blender. Although the frying of the ingredients may seem a little complicated, you won't need to change the pan or the oil if you follow the specific order of the steps. Serve the dish with Arroz Blanco and corn tortillas.

*6 chicken thighs and leg quarters, skin on*
*Vegetable oil for frying*
*1 teaspoon sesame seeds, toasted*

### Blackberry Mole
Makes 2 quarts.

*2 ancho chiles* ✽
*2 mulato chiles* ✽
*3 pasilla chiles* ✽
*1½ tablespoons reserved chile seeds*
*8 to 12 tablespoons vegetable oil plus additional as needed*
*2 heaping tablespoons raw skinless peanuts*
*15 whole raw almonds*
*2 heaping tablespoons raw, hulled pumpkin seeds* ✽
*2 heaping tablespoons pecan pieces*

*Quarter of a small white onion*
*2 garlic cloves, peeled*
*3 tablespoons unhulled sesame seeds*
*⅛ teaspoon anise seeds*
*⅛ teaspoon coriander seeds*
*1½-inch piece of a Mexican cinnamon stick* ✽
*1 pinch ground cloves*
*1 pinch ground cumin*
*1 pinch dried Mexican oregano*
*Half of a 6-inch corn tortilla*
*2 tablespoons vegetable oil*
*4½ cups Basic Chicken Broth* ✤
*2 pints fresh ripe blackberries*
*3 tablespoons sugar*
*1 ounce Mexican chocolate, grated* ✽
*1½ teaspoons sea salt or to taste*

Prepare the Blackberry Mole. Remove any stems from the chiles. Slit each chile lengthwise and scrape out all the seeds and veins, reserving 1½ tablespoons of the seeds.

In a small frying pan, heat 3 tablespoons of the oil over medium heat. Fry the peanuts and almonds together until the peanuts are a golden color. With a slotted spoon, transfer to a large mixing bowl. Fry the pumpkin seeds until they swell and stop popping; transfer to the mixing bowl. Fry the pecans long enough to lightly roast them; transfer to the bowl. Fry each chile on both sides until the inside flesh has turned dark brown, about 15 seconds; be careful not to burn them. Transfer to the bowl. Fry onion and garlic together until lightly browned; transfer to the bowl. Add more oil as needed. Mix reserved chile seeds, sesame seeds, anise seeds, coriander seeds, and cinnamon and fry in the same oil until sesame seeds are lightly toasted. Just before removing the seeds and spices from the oil, add the ground cloves, cumin, and oregano; fry a few seconds more. Transfer to the bowl with the other ingredients and set aside.

Using tongs, toast the tortilla directly over a low flame, turning constantly until large burned spots form. Crumble, mix with the fried ingredients, and transfer to a blender. Add 3 cups of the chicken broth and blend to a smooth but textured puree.

Heat 2 tablespoons of the oil in a 3-quart saucepan over medium heat and add the puree (be careful—it will splatter). Reduce heat to low and cook, stirring constantly to prevent sticking, for 8 to 10 minutes. Remove from heat and set aside.

Add blackberries, sugar, and ¼ cup of the chicken broth to the blender and puree. Strain the blackberry puree over the sauce, discarding the seeds. Add 1 cup of the broth. Simmer sauce for 15 minutes, stirring occasionally. Add chocolate and simmer an additional 15 minutes, or until small pools of oil form around the bubbles. This means the mole has fully cooked—or, as they say in Mexico, the sauce has "seasoned." Remove from heat and add salt.

Heat oil in a heavy, 12-inch skillet over medium-high heat. Sear chicken pieces about 8 to 9 minutes, or until golden brown, turning once. Reduce heat to low and pour Blackberry Mole over the chicken; cover and cook for 20 minutes, adding the remaining ¼ cup of stock if needed. (The consistency should be like a thin gravy.) Garnish with toasted sesame seeds. Serves 8.

# MOLE VERDE CON CHOCHOYONES
## Green Mole with Masa Dumplings and Chicken

Mexican native Patricia Quintana, a longtime friend of Tom and Miguel's, has represented her country as a culinary ambassador for many years. This is an adaptation of her recipe for traditional green mole that appeared in her second book, *Mexico—Feasts of Life*. Mole Verde is an everyday dish in the central and southern regions of Mexico.

*2 pounds boneless, skinless chicken breasts
   or chicken tenders, cut into 2-inch
   chunks*

*Half of a medium white onion, cut into
   chunks*

*1 celery stalk, cut into chunks*

*1 carrot, cut into chunks*

*1 teaspoon sea salt*

*Arroz Blanco* ❖

## Mole Verde
Makes 4 to 5 cups.

*1 cup hulled pumpkin seeds, toasted* ✿

*¼ teaspoon cumin seeds, toasted*

*10 whole black peppercorns*

*5 cups reserved chicken broth*

*2 leaves romaine lettuce*

*1 bunch radish leaves*

*6 sprigs fresh cilantro*

*4 sprigs fresh epazote* ✿

*Half of a medium white onion, chopped*

*3 garlic cloves, chopped*

*4 serrano chiles, chopped* ✿

*4 to 5 tomatillos, husked, cooked, and
   drained, or 1 cup canned tomatillos* ✿

*2 tablespoons vegetable oil or lard*

## Masa Dumplings

*1½ cups masa harina, prepared according
   to directions on package*

*3 tablespoons vegetable shortening or lard*

*1 teaspoon sea salt*

*½ teaspoon ground black pepper*

*2 tablespoons chopped cilantro*

*2 tablespoons chopped epazote* ✿

*Quarter of a medium white onion, minced*

In a 3-quart saucepan, combine chicken pieces, vegetables, and salt; add water to cover and bring to a boil. Reduce heat to a simmer and cook until chicken is tender, about 20 minutes. Remove the chicken and refrigerate. Discard the vegetables, reserving the chicken broth; set aside.

Prepare the Mole Verde. Combine seeds and peppercorns in a spice grinder and process to a powder. Transfer to a small bowl, combine with 1 cup of the reserved chicken broth, and set aside. Combine romaine leaves, radish leaves, cilantro, epazote, onion, garlic, chiles, and tomatillos in a blender. Add the spiced broth and 1 additional cup of the reserved chicken broth; puree. (This may have to be done in two batches.) Heat oil in a heavy Dutch oven or soup pot over medium heat. Add puree and cook for about 10 minutes, stirring often to prevent sticking.

While the sauce is cooking, prepare the Masa Dumplings. In the mixing bowl of a stand mixer, beat the prepared masa with the remaining ingredients until light and fluffy. Form the dough into 1-inch balls and make a deep indentation in the center so each ball resembles a tiny bowl; set aside.

Add the reserved chicken to the hot Mole Verde; add 2 to 3 cups of the reserved broth. When the sauce returns to a simmer, gently add the dumplings. Cover and poach dumplings for 10 to 12 minutes. Serve with Arroz Blanco. Serves 6 to 8.

## Wine Suggestion
Burgundian Chardonnay

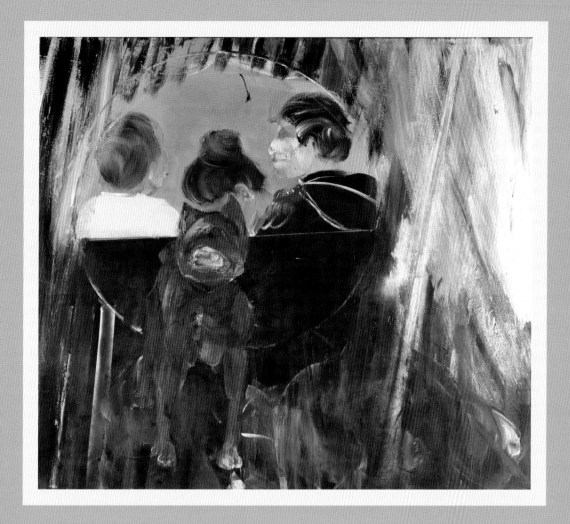

## Sergio Rodríguez Terry

*Red Dog*, circa 1987. Oil, 65½ × 74½ inches.

*Rodríguez is from Mexico but now lives and paints in Austin. I think his brooding style resembles that of Francis Bacon. He has written that he wants his "painting to come instantly and immediately, so that in the end, there is no idea to be interpreted, rather a thing to be experienced." Having experienced this particular painting, we lovingly named it* Red Dog.

T.G.

## Francisco Ochoa

*Ensayo con el sub.* 24 × 18 inches.

*Ochoa was a Mexican artist who began his career as an accountant. Fortunately for the art world, the Galería Estela Shapiro was an early client, and when the proprietor discovered his talent for painting, she organized a one-man show.* Ensayo con el sub *whimsically illustrates the "chorus line"—the dance between the principal participants in the Chiapas Zapatista movement—from left to right: society lady, indigenous person, Zapata, Subcommandante Marcos, the Bishop of Chiapas, Marcos's companion, and the subversive cat.*

T.G.

# ZARAPE DE PATO
## Stacked Enchiladas with Duck

This eclectic enchilada preparation was developed by Roberto Santibáñez during his tenure as Fonda San Miguel's chef and was subsequently re-created by Miguel. The recipe's title refers to the serape-like layers of tortilla that provide a protective covering for the succulent duck breast.

*2 to 4 tablespoons safflower oil*

*4 8-ounce duck breasts, skin left on*

*1 teaspoon sea salt*

*8 corn tortillas*

*¼ cup vegetable oil*

*½ cup Frijoles Refritos* ❖

*2 large tomatoes, broiled, skinned, and chopped (optional)* ✽

*Pasilla chiles, toasted and shredded* ✽

*Cilantro sprigs for garnish*

### Cilantro-Poblano Sauce

Makes 3 to 3½ cups.

*5 poblano chiles, roasted, peeled, seeded, deveined, and chopped* ✽

*1½ cups Basic Chicken Stock* ❖

*¼ pound fresh spinach, blanched in boiling water and pressed to remove excess moisture (about ¼ cup spinach)*

*½ cup cilantro leaves, loosely packed*

*2 teaspoons coarse sea salt or to taste*

*1½ cups heavy cream*

Prepare the Cilantro-Poblano Sauce. In a blender, combine all sauce ingredients except the cream. Blend until very smooth. Transfer to a heavy, 2-quart, nonreactive saucepan and bring to a rolling boil. Whisk in cream and return to a boil. Immediately remove from direct heat (if overcooked, the sauce will turn dark green). Keep warm.

To prepare the duck breasts, heat the safflower oil in a heavy skillet over medium heat. Fry duck breasts, skin side down, for 3 minutes. Turn, sprinkle with salt, and fry an additional 3 minutes for medium-rare. Remove from heat and drain on paper towels. Slice each breast in several diagonal slices. Keep hot.

To prepare the tortillas, heat the vegetable oil in a small skillet until the surface of the oil shimmers. Lightly fry each tortilla just until soft, about 15 seconds on each side. Transfer to a tray lined with paper towels.

To assemble, spread 1 tablespoon of the Frijoles Refritos on each tortilla. Ladle a generous pool of warm Cilantro-Poblano Sauce on each of 4 dinner plates and place a tortilla, with beans facing up, in the pool of sauce. Arrange a fan of hot duck slices on top of the beans. Sprinkle with chopped tomatoes, if desired. Cover the meat with another tortilla, beans facing down. Ladle a generous portion of the warm Cilantro-Poblano Sauce over the entire stack. Decorate with shreds of pasilla chiles and garnish with fresh cilantro sprigs. Serves 4.

### Wine Suggestion

Barbera d'Alba

# HUACHINANGO VERACRUZANO ✿
## Red Snapper, Veracruz Style

Few Mexican dishes are more recognizable than this delicious fish from the coastal state of Veracruz. The Spanish influence is evident in the use of olive oil, olives, and capers. The sauce is wonderful whether you serve it with whole fish, fillets, or shrimp. Miguel serves this dish with Arroz Blanco and Frijoles Negros.

*6 6- to 7-ounce red snapper fillets, skinned*

*2 tablespoons olive oil*

*Sea salt and ground black pepper to taste*

*12 thin slices fresh lime, about 3 limes*

### Veracruzano Sauce
Makes 5 cups.

*¼ cup olive oil*

*1 medium white onion, thinly sliced*

*3 garlic cloves, chopped*

*6 medium tomatoes, diced and seeded*

*2 bay leaves*

*½ teaspoon dried Mexican oregano*

*15 pitted green olives, cut in half*

*2 tablespoons large capers, drained*

*2 to 3 pickled jalapeños (depending on desired level of heat), drained, seeded, and cut into ¼-inch strips* ✿

*Sea salt to taste*

Prepare the Veracruzano Sauce. In a heavy nonreactive pan, heat olive oil over medium heat. Cook onion and garlic until soft, about 3 minutes. Add tomatoes and remaining ingredients and cook for about 10 minutes over low heat, stirring often. Keep the sauce warm while you prepare the fish.

Preheat oven to broil. Place oven rack 4 inches below heat source. Brush each fillet with olive oil and a sprinkling of salt and pepper. Place on a greased baking sheet and broil for 4 to 5 minutes, just until the fish is opaque but still firm. Do not overcook. Place each fillet on a warm plate, top with a generous serving of the Veracruzano Sauce, and garnish with 2 lime slices. Serves 6.

### Wine Suggestion

Chianti Classico (Sangiovese)

### Variations

Peel and devein 36 shrimp (21–25 count), leaving tails on. Sauté in olive oil until shrimp begin to turn pink, about 4 to 5 minutes. Serve 6 shrimp per person on a bed of Arroz Blanco with a generous serving of Veracruzano Sauce. Serves 6.

Substitute a 3- to 4-pound whole fish (pictured) for the fillets. Preheat oven to 375 degrees. Rub fish inside and out with olive oil, salt, and pepper. Score the sides of the fish on the diagonal. In a large nonreactive oval baking dish, pour a third of the Veracruzano Sauce in the bottom and lay the prepared fish on top. Cover with the remaining sauce. Bake 30 to 40 minutes or until the flesh flakes when tested with a fork. Serve on a platter surrounded by parsley and lime wedges. Serves 4 to 6.

# PESCADO TIKIN XIK ❊

## Fish with Achiote Rub

The same achiote paste that gives an earthy flavor to Yucatan barbecue dishes such as Cochinita Pibil and Agujas de Res imparts brilliant color to this fish preparation, which is also from the Yucatan. Though snapper is classic, the dish can also be made with black drum, trout, or tilapia, with sides of Arroz Blanco and Frijoles Negros. Served cold with Chipotle Mayonnaise, it is a great snack to take along on a picnic. At the Hacienda Sunday Brunch Buffet it is always a favorite on the cold appetizer table.

*6 6- to 7-ounce red snapper fillets, skinned*

*Achiote Rub (see recipe for Cochinita Pibil)*

*Cebollas Rojas en Escabeche (see separate recipe)*

Preheat oven to broil. Place oven rack 4 inches below heat source. Lightly grease a baking sheet large enough to hold all the fillets. Gently rub each fillet on both sides with the Achiote Rub. (Reserve any remaining rub for another use.) Place fillets on the prepared baking sheet and broil in preheated oven for 5 to 7 minutes, or until fish is opaque but still firm. Do not overcook. Remove from broiler, garnish with Cebollas Rojas en Escabeche, and serve warm. Serves 6.

## Wine Suggestion

Oregon Pinot Noir

## Variation

To serve cold, chill thoroughly. Garnish with the Cebollas Rojas en Escabeche and serve with chilled Chipotle Mayonnaise (see recipe for Calamares).

Arnulfo Mendoza

*El camarón dorado, 1995.*
Oil on gouache,
16 × 19½ inches.

*This small but exquisite painting, which gets its subtle burnished effect from gold leaf, is just one example of the diverse art of Arnulfo Mendoza of Oaxaca. It's also very indicative of a certain school of Oaxacan painting. Oaxaca is a very mystical place, and Oaxacan artists paint with unusual colors and great feeling. Arnulfo, who died in 2014, was the husband of Mary Jane Gagnier-Mendoza, and together they owned one of Mexico's most unique galleries, La Mano Mágica in Oaxaca. Arnulfo was not only a painter but also one of Mexico's best-known weavers. His birthplace, the village of Teotitlan, outside of the city of Oaxaca, is known as the village of weavers. Arnulfo had shown his weavings and paintings all over the world. Fonda San Miguel was pleased to loan a large and important weaving to the Mexican Fine Arts Museum of Chicago for a show featuring Arnulfo's work. Many years ago, Arnulfo designed the menu for Fonda San Miguel, and our most recent menu incorporates art from previous menus designed by Arnulfo and other artists.*

*T.G.*

# CAMARONES AL MOJO DE AJO
## Shrimp in Garlic Sauce

The pleasant crunch of fried garlic against the rich mellow garlic-butter sauce in this recipe is a perfect complement to grilled seafood, whether it is Gulf shrimp, redfish, soft-shell crabs, or pretty much anything you would choose. Fried garlic is an integral part of seafood dishes from the Gulf Coast of Mexico. It is as good with Italian pasta (such as spaghetti with olive oil and garlic) as it is with Mexican seafood. It keeps well in an air-tight container and does not have to be refrigerated. The restaurant's sous chef, Oscar Álvarez, describes this as his favorite dish to cook for himself. You couldn't ask for a better recommendation!

> *¾ cup butter*
>
> *3 garlic cloves, thinly sliced*
>
> *⅓ cup olive oil*
>
> *36 raw shrimp (21–25 count), peeled and deveined*
>
> *Chopped fresh parsley leaves for garnish*
>
> *Arroz Blanco* ❖

### Fried Garlic

Makes ½ cup.

> *1 cup vegetable oil*
>
> *¾ cup minced garlic*

Prepare the Fried Garlic. In a heavy, 10-inch skillet, heat the oil over high heat until the oil is shimmering but not smoking. Add garlic, reduce heat to medium-low, and cook 10 to 15 minutes, or until golden brown, stirring often. (Be careful not to burn it.) Remove garlic from the oil with a slotted spoon, strain through a fine strainer, and drain on paper towels.

In a small saucepan, melt the butter over medium heat; add the sliced garlic, reduce heat to low, and keep warm on top of the stove. Do not brown the garlic. In a nonreactive skillet or sauté pan, heat the olive oil over medium-high heat and sauté the shrimp until they curl and turn pink, about 4 to 5 minutes. Divide the shrimp among 6 dinner plates and spoon the warm garlic-butter sauce over each serving. Sprinkle with Fried Garlic and chopped parsley. Serve with Arroz Blanco. Serves 6.

### Wine Suggestion

Pinot Grigio

### Variation

Substitute 6 6- to 7-ounce fillets of a firm fish (such as redfish, drum, or tilapia). Broil, grill, or sauté the fish and proceed as directed.

# FINE WINE WITH MEXICAN FOOD?
## ¡Claro que sí!

Wine with Mexican food? That was a preposterous question in 1972 when Miguel and I opened San Angel restaurant in Houston. Wine was not even considered an option. It was all margaritas and beer. Even in Mexico's finest restaurants, Mexican food was typically not served with fine wines in those days.

But there we were, attempting to persuade our patrons that they should drink wine with our food. And what a wine list it was! We offered Schramsberg, Joseph Heitz, Concannon, Chappellet, Beaulieu Cabernet Sauvignon Reserve, most of the Ridge Zinfandels. San Angel was one of the only restaurants in Texas to offer an exclusively California wine list. We later experimented with South American wines, even Hungarian wines. We really went far out with Dr. Konstantin Frank's wines from the Finger Lakes region of New York. Were we crazy? Charlie Finkel, a Houston wine impresario as well as a wine educator and writer, produced for us a quirky, entertaining wine list. Alas, it was lost in the move.

After Fonda San Miguel was fairly well established, we invited John Roegnik of the Austin Wine Merchant to brainstorm ways to promote wine with Mexican food. Julio Michaud of Mexico City, a renowned wine writer, came to the Hill Country Food and Wine Festival, then a fledgling event, to serve on a wine seminar with John and me to discuss the outlandish idea of pairing wine with Mexican food. Patricia Quintana served the food.

Despite an enthusiastic reception at the festival, the concept was still a hard sell at the restaurant. Our patrons

would say, "Wine? Next time, maybe—tonight I'll have a margarita and my husband wants a Corona!"

As a last-ditch effort, we tried bribery—or rather, low pricing, which was mostly unheard of in restaurants. Oenophiles thought the wine list contained typographical errors and rushed to order wine before the mistakes were discovered. We installed an expensive Cruvinet—the first in an Austin restaurant—so that we could offer many more wines by the glass, especially red wine, served at the correct temperature.

Happily I can report that Fonda San Miguel has quadrupled its wine sales and received four *Wine Spectator* Awards for its wine lists in as many years since submitting our list for competition. The minimal markup doesn't please our CPA, but sorry, sir, it's the experience we're after!

Mexican food and wine work as well together as most any food and wine do. But a notion has always prevailed that the beverage to drink with Mexican food must deal with the spiciness and the heat (although not all Mexican dishes rely on spice or chiles to make their point—can we agree on that?). For many, beer has been the beverage of choice, something to refresh, to "wash it back." As a beverage to complement fine cuisine, however, beer doesn't always cut it. While beer may aid psychologically, it does little more than cool the tongue. Beer just doesn't work the same way that wine does in clearing the palate.

Without going off the deep end in a scientific discussion, I think it's safe to say that a beverage should serve both as refreshment and as a foil for the cuisine. Otherwise, the food begins to lose its flavor and appeal. The interplay of fruit and acidity in a fine wine sets up the tongue, the palate, for greater appreciation.

For some, champagne or a sparkling wine is a natural extension of what beer would otherwise accomplish. For many dishes, a white wine that shows its fruit (as opposed to stern structure or "oakiness") can be the best choice. For example, an Oregon Pinot Gris by, say, Chehalem actually assuages the tongue texturally and, at the same time, imparts its own special flavor and teases with gentle astringency. Sauvignon Blancs from various sources, such as the United States and New Zealand, are recommended. Pinot Grigios are likewise excellent. And there are many wonderful Italian and Spanish white wines, of course.

For many, the first duty of a fine wine is to be red. Why shouldn't a fine Cabernet Sauvignon or Zinfandel be served with Carne Asada (beef tenderloin), *chuletas* (pork chops), or *cordero* (lamb)? Pinot Noir goes quite well with Cochinita Pibil (the Yucatecan pork specialty) and is a nice red wine that crosses over well with milder, non-beef dishes. For example, Pinot Noirs are enjoyable with Pescado Tikin Xik (the achiote-marinated fish recipe).

The point of all this: Mexican cuisine needs fine wines every bit as much as any other ethnic cuisine that is commonly served with wine.

T.G.

## Bob Wade

*Xochimilco*, 2000.
Colorized photograph on linen, 43 × 72 inches.
© bobwade.com

*I found this piece at Spazio, a contemporary gallery in Austin, and I knew right away that the restaurant had the perfect spot for it. Of all the art acquired for the restaurant over the years, this is the first piece that wasn't an actual painting. Xochimilco is an old photograph of what is commonly known as the Floating Gardens of Mexico City—part of the ancient canal system from the Aztec era. The piece has a luminosity, almost a 3-D effect, which comes from Wade's magic. A native Austinite, Bob Wade has made a specialty of hand-tinting vintage black-and-white photographs. He enlarges them, transfers them to photo-sensitive linen, and then brings them to life with airbrushing. His series of cowgirls is especially well known. He is also a sculptor, and created the huge forty-foot boots displayed at the entrance to San Antonio's North Star Mall as well as the dancing frogs, which returned to their original location in Dallas in 2014 after many years at Carl's Corner, an I-35 truck stop near Hillsboro.*

*T.G.*

HACIENDA BUFFET

Fonda San Miguel's Hacienda Sunday Brunch Buffet is consistently rated the best in Austin. Buffet service began in 1985 and quickly developed into a festive Sunday event where customers come to relax amid the museum-quality folk art collection and sample a mouth-watering assortment of Mexican regional dishes. The most popular aspect of the buffet by far is Miguel's genial presence at the table. Customers obviously enjoy his anecdotes about the histories of the different dishes and actively seek his recommendations. Regular interaction with a satisfied clientele is the high point of his week.

# SAN MIGUEL OMELET

Long before San Miguel became famous for its Hacienda Sunday Brunch Buffet, the restaurant offered an à la carte brunch menu featuring several egg dishes, including Huevos Motuleños and this delicious omelet. The filling for the omelet is based on the restaurant's unique Chile con Queso appetizer. Serve the omelet with a side of Frijoles Refritos, fresh tropical fruit, and plenty of warm tortillas.

> *2 tablespoons butter*
>
> *6 eggs*
>
> *¼ cup milk*
>
> *1 teaspoon sea salt*
>
> *½ teaspoon ground black pepper*
>
> *Chile con Queso Filling (see below)*

## Chile con Queso Filling

Makes 1½ cups.

> *3 tablespoons vegetable oil*
>
> *Half of a medium white onion, sliced*
>
> *6 poblano chiles, roasted, peeled, seeded, and cut into ¼-inch strips* ✽
>
> *Half of a medium tomato, peeled, seeded, and chopped* ✽
>
> *Scant ½ cup milk*
>
> *1 cup shredded Monterey Jack or Muenster cheese*
>
> *½ teaspoon sea salt*

Prepare the Chile con Queso Filling. Heat oil in a heavy, 3-quart saucepan over medium-high heat. Add onion and cook until wilted and transparent, but not browned, about 3 to 5 minutes. Add chiles and tomato; cook for 6 to 10 minutes. Add milk and cook an additional 3 minutes. Add cheese and salt, stirring until cheese melts. Keep warm while preparing the omelet.

In a 10-inch nonstick omelet pan, melt the butter over medium heat until foamy. Break the eggs into a bowl and whisk together with milk, salt, and pepper until smooth and well blended. Pour egg mixture into the hot butter and gently tip the skillet so that the egg mixture covers the entire skillet bottom. Use a spatula to move the mixture around so that the entire surface begins to set. When the eggs are almost set, fill the center of the omelet with the warm Chile con Queso Filling. Use a spatula to gently roll half the omelet over to cover the filling. Remove from heat. Slide the omelet onto a serving platter and cut into 4 portions. Serves 4.

# HUEVOS RANCHEROS
## Ranch-Style Eggs

The smoky flavor of the roasted sauce makes this "ranch hands" egg dish a popular breakfast in northern Mexico and across the American Southwest. The sauce alone makes a good table sauce for dipping with tortilla chips. The classic sides for Huevos Rancheros are Frijoles Refritos and plenty of fresh tortillas.

*12 eggs*
*Oil for frying*

### Salsa Ranchera

Makes 4 cups.

*4 large tomatoes, roasted until blistered* ✿

*Half of a medium white onion, chopped*

*2 to 4 serrano chiles, roasted until blistered and chopped* ✿

*1 garlic clove, chopped*

*Sea salt to taste*

*1 tablespoon vegetable oil*

Prepare the Salsa Ranchera. Combine all sauce ingredients except the oil in a *molcajete* or food processor and puree. In a heavy, 12-inch skillet, heat the oil over medium heat. Add the tomato mixture (be careful—it will splatter), reduce heat to low, and cook for about 5 minutes. Keep warm.

In a large, heavy skillet, heat oil over medium heat and fry the eggs. Serve 2 eggs on each plate with a generous portion of the Salsa Ranchera. Serves 6.

# HUEVOS MOTULEÑOS ✿
## Eggs, Motul Style

Huevos Motuleños, eggs stacked with tortillas and black beans, are often referred to as "Mexican Eggs Benedict." The hearty breakfast dish is reputed to come from the pueblo of Motul, outside Mérida in the Yucatan Peninsula. Regardless of its origins, it is a delightful way to start the day. Fonda San Miguel was the first restaurant in Austin to present this dish, always with poached eggs. The dish can be made with fried eggs as well.

*12 eggs, poached or fried*

*2 tablespoons vegetable oil or lard*

*12 corn tortillas*

*2 cups Frijoles Refritos* ✥

*Tomato Sauce (see below)*

*1 cup (4 ounces) shredded Monterey Jack cheese*

*⅓ pound ham, cut into small cubes*

*⅔ cup frozen green peas, thawed*

## Tomato Sauce

Makes 5 cups.

*7 large tomatoes, roasted until blistered* ✽

*2 serrano chiles* ✽

*1 garlic clove, chopped*

*3 tablespoons vegetable oil*

*Half of a medium white onion, chopped*

*Sea salt and ground black pepper to taste*

Prepare the Tomato Sauce. Combine the tomatoes, chiles, and garlic in a blender; blend well. In a heavy, 12-inch deep-sided skillet or Dutch oven, heat the oil over medium heat and sauté the onion until wilted and transparent, about 3 to 4 minutes. Add the tomato mixture (be careful—it will splatter). Cook over medium heat for 8 to 10 minutes, stirring often. Keep warm.

In a heavy, 10-inch skillet, heat the oil over medium heat until it shimmers. Using tongs to hold the edges, fry each tortilla for about 10 seconds until soft and pliable. Drain on paper towels and keep warm. On each of 6 warm plates, place a tortilla and spread with ⅓ cup Frijoles Refritos. Place 2 cooked eggs on each tortilla; cover with a tortilla. Spoon a generous serving of Tomato Sauce over each tortilla and sprinkle with shredded cheese, ham cubes, and peas. Serve warm. Serves 6.

NOTE: Here is an old restaurant trick for perfect poached eggs. Poach the eggs in advance. Using a skimmer or slotted spoon, transfer them to a bucket of ice water. Right before serving, bring a small pot of salted water to a boil and dip the eggs in the boiling water just long enough to warm them through.

For fried eggs, fry the eggs lightly and transfer to an oiled baking sheet and hold in a warm oven for no longer than 10 to 15 minutes.

# HUEVOS EN RABO DE MESTIZA

## Eggs Poached in Chile Tomato Broth

In Spanish, "rabo" is sometimes used to mean raggedy clothing. A "mestiza" is a Mexican woman of mixed Spanish/indigenous heritage. Hence, "rabo de mestiza" means a mestiza woman's rags! The combined ingredients of this dish could look like that, if your imagination stretches that far.

*3 poblano chiles*

*⅓ cup cooking oil*

*Half of a white onion, finely chopped*

*2 garlic cloves, minced*

*7 red, ripe tomatoes, roasted, peeled, and chopped*

*2 cups chicken broth (see separate recipe)*

*Salt to taste*

*12 whole eggs*

*½ cup crumbled queso fresco for garnish*

Toast the chiles directly over an open flame, on the broiler, or on a griddle to char the skins. When well blistered and charred, put the chiles in a plastic bag to sweat them for about 10 minutes. Then remove the loosened skin with paper towels. Don't peel the chiles under running water; the water flushes out all of their flavor. Split the chiles open and remove seeds and veins. Cut the chiles in ¼-inch wide strips.

In a saucepan, heat the oil over medium heat and fry the onions, garlic, and tomatoes, stirring constantly until the mixture forms a thick paste. Add the chicken broth, chiles, and salt to taste. Cook over low heat until the mixture comes to a boil. Remove from heat and set aside for later use.

When ready to serve, bring the sauce to a boil once again. Drop raw eggs into the hot sauce, one by one, poaching them to the degree of doneness you prefer (usually around 4 minutes).

To serve, place two poached eggs per serving in the bottom of an individual bowl. Top with tomato sauce and chile strips. Garnish with the crumbled queso fresco.

Serve with hot corn tortillas. Serves 6.

# HUEVOS REVUELTOS CON MIGAS
## Scrambled Eggs with Tortillas and Cheese

*Migas* are the quintessential Mexican breakfast dish in Texas, and you're likely to find as many subtle differences in the preparations as in the cooks who make them. They are always a popular item on the Hacienda Sunday Brunch Buffet and vary slightly depending on which of the cooks makes them. Some cooks use poblano chiles, some use jalapeños, and every now and then someone throws in some chipotles for extra spice. Try the recipe and then customize it to your family's palate. Salsa de Chile Pasilla or Salsa Mexicana is especially good with this dish.

*2 corn tortillas, cut into small squares*

*¼ cup vegetable oil*

*12 eggs*

*1 teaspoon sea salt*

*1 poblano chile, roasted, peeled, seeded, and chopped* ✽

*1 medium white onion, diced*

*1 medium tomato, seeded and diced*

*1 cup (4 ounces) shredded Monterey Jack cheese*

In a heavy, 12-inch skillet, heat the oil over medium heat and fry the tortilla pieces until they are golden brown and crisp, about 3 to 4 minutes. Using a skimmer or slotted spatula, remove and drain on paper towels. Keep oil hot. Break the eggs into a bowl, whisk together with a fork, and add the salt. Pour the beaten eggs into the hot skillet and quickly add the tortilla pieces, chile, onion, tomato, and cheese. Scramble eggs to the desired level of doneness. Serve with your favorite salsa. Serves 6.

# HUEVOS CON CHORIZO
## Scrambled Eggs with Mexican Sausage

Mexican chorizo sausages vary in the amount of spice and fat they contain, so you may want to sample several brands before you find one that appeals to your family. This dish is equally at home in a chafing dish on a brunch buffet or as a tasty filling for handy homemade breakfast tacos made with flour tortillas.

*⅓ cup vegetable oil*

*4 4-inch Mexican chorizo sausages, skinned and crumbled* ✿

*Half of a large white onion, chopped*

*1 large tomato, chopped*

*4 serrano chiles, chopped* ✿

*8 eggs*

*1 teaspoon sea salt*

*Salsa Mexicana* ❖

*Frijoles Refritos* ❖

In a medium to large skillet, heat the oil and cook chorizo over medium heat for about 5 minutes to brown the meat and render the fat. Drain all but 3 tablespoons of fat from the skillet. Return skillet to medium heat and add onion, tomato, and chiles. Cook for about 5 minutes, or until the onion is wilted and transparent.

While the sausage mixture is cooking, break the eggs into a bowl and whisk together with salt. Pour the eggs into the skillet and scramble eggs to the desired level of doneness. Serve on a platter garnished with Salsa Mexicana and a side of Frijoles Refritos. Serves 6.

## Rufino Tamayo

*Sandías*, ca. 1980.
Mixograph on handmade paper,
29 × 37 inches.

*Sandías by Rufino Tamayo is perhaps the restaurant's most famous piece of art, so it occupies a prominent wall. People comment on it frequently and always seem to remember it, for the two bright red watermelons make a lasting impression. This print is a very special type of mixograph. The artist made the print himself on paper that he had made by hand. At the time when I was pursuing this print, I first became acquainted with Dana Ravel and discovered her Galerie Ravel in Austin. I had seen the print in a gallery in Santa Fe and had put a hold on it. But soon after I returned to Austin, I met Dana and told her about it. She said, "Dear, I can get that for you. How much do they want for it?" I told her the price, and she said she could do better. So I canceled the order and bought the print from Dana. Tamayo made about fifty copies of this watermelon print, but it's very hard to come by one these days unless you purchase it from an individual collector. Tamayo was influenced by Picasso, and you see stylistic similarities to Picasso in the paintings of the younger artist. When Tamayo died in 1991 and lay in state at the Palacio de Bellas Artes in Mexico City, millions of people came to pay their respects. He is one of Mexico's best-known painters internationally, equal in stature to Diego Rivera and Frida Kahlo.*

*T.G.*

# CHILAQUILES DE GUAJOLOTE ✿
## Tortilla Casserole with Turkey

This tortilla casserole is a great holiday dish to prepare when you want to use up leftovers. Miguel uses shredded leftover turkey as well as whatever vegetables remain from the holiday feast. It is a reliable dish for brunches or luncheons, paired with a seasonal salad. The tangy tomatillo sauce in this dish can also be used in recipes for other chilaquiles as well as Enchiladas Verdes. Though often referred to as "green tomatoes," tomatillos are members of the gooseberry family.

*¾ cup plus 1 tablespoon corn oil*

*18 corn tortillas*

*3 medium zucchini, thinly sliced*

*2 cups chayote or other squash, thinly sliced*

*1 cup fresh or thawed frozen corn kernels*

*2 cups green beans, steamed and cut into 1-inch pieces*

*2 to 3 cups leftover turkey, shredded*

*2 cups (8 ounces) shredded Monterey Jack or panela cheese* ✿

*6 cups Salsa de Tomatillo (see below)*

*2 cups sour cream*

*1 tablespoon milk*

*Sea salt and ground black pepper to taste*

### Salsa de Tomatillo

Makes 5 to 6 cups.

*60 tomatillos, husked and rinsed (about 3 pounds)* ✿

*8 serrano chiles (seeded and deveined for a milder dish)* ✿

*4 cups water*

*5 garlic cloves, chopped*

*1 cup coarsely chopped cilantro leaves*

*2 tablespoons vegetable oil*

*Sea salt to taste*

Prepare the Salsa de Tomatillo. In a heavy, 6-quart, non-reactive saucepan over medium-high heat, combine tomatillos, chiles, and water; bring to a boil. Reduce heat to low and simmer until the tomatillos are tender, about 10 to 12 minutes. Drain, reserving ½ to 1 cup of the cooking liquid. Working in batches, combine tomatillos, chiles, reserved cooking liquid, garlic, and cilantro in a blender and blend to a smooth puree. In a heavy, 12-inch, deep-sided skillet, heat the oil over medium heat and cook the tomatillo mixture for about 10 minutes, stirring often. Add salt to taste.

Prepare the casserole. In a heavy, 10-inch skillet, heat ¾ cup of the corn oil over medium heat until the oil shimmers. Using tongs, submerge the tortillas, one at a time, in the hot oil for about 10 seconds (the tortillas should remain pliable). Transfer to a baking sheet lined with paper towels to drain. Lightly oil a 13-by-9-inch baking dish and set aside. In a heavy, 12-inch, nonstick skillet, heat the remaining 1 tablespoon of oil over medium heat until shimmering. Add both kinds of squash and cook over medium heat about 5 minutes. Add the corn and green beans and cook until just tender, about 2 to 3 minutes. Add salt and pepper to taste.

Preheat oven to 375 degrees. Arrange 6 of the softened tortillas in the prepared baking dish, overlapping the edges. Cover with half of the shredded turkey, half of the vegetable mixture, 1 cup of the cheese, 1 cup of the Salsa de Tomatillo, and ¾ cup of the sour cream. Repeat the layering process with 6 additional tortillas, the remaining turkey, vegetable mixture, and cheese, 1 cup of the Salsa de Tomatillo, and ¾ cup of the sour cream. Top with the remaining 6 tortillas. Drizzle with 1 cup of the Salsa de Tomatillo, cover with foil, and bake in preheated oven for about 50 minutes, or until heated through.

During the last few minutes of the cooking time, heat the remaining 3 cups Salsa de Tomatillo over low heat and keep warm. In a small bowl, whisk together the remaining ½ cup sour cream and the milk; drizzle over the hot casserole when it comes out of the oven. Serve the hot casserole with hot Salsa de Tomatillo on the side. Serves 8.

# CHILAQUILES EN SALSA DE CHILE PASILLA
## Tortilla Casserole with Pasilla Sauce

This hearty casserole, a popular dish on the Hacienda Sunday Brunch Buffet, is just the right complement to *migas* or Huevos Rancheros. The basic recipe calls for Salsa de Chile Pasilla, a rust-colored sauce that is good with many egg dishes, so save extra sauce to brighten up another breakfast. You can vary this casserole with your choice of sauces.

> ¾ *cup corn oil*
>
> *18 day-old corn tortillas, cut into quarters*
>
> *4 cups shredded Monterey Jack or panela cheese* ✽
>
> *3 cups Salsa de Pasilla (see below)*
>
> ½ *cup sour cream*
>
> *3 tablespoons milk*

### Salsa de Chile Pasilla

Makes 4 to 5 cups.

> *16 pasilla chiles, seeds and stems removed* ✽
>
> *4 garlic cloves*
>
> *2 teaspoons sea salt*
>
> *3 to 4 cups water*
>
> *4 tablespoons vegetable oil or lard*

Prepare the Salsa de Chile Pasilla. Using a hot comal or griddle, toast the chiles for about 10 seconds on each side. Combine the toasted chiles, garlic, salt, and water in a blender and puree until smooth. Heat the vegetable oil in a heavy skillet over medium heat until it shimmers. Add the chile puree (be careful—it will splatter). Cook over medium heat, stirring constantly, for about 5 minutes. Set aside.

Prepare the casserole. In a small skillet, heat corn oil over moderate heat until the oil shimmers. Using tongs and working in batches, submerge a few of the tortilla quarters in the hot oil for about 10 seconds (tortillas should remain pliable). Remove with a skimmer or slotted spatula and drain on a baking sheet lined with paper towels. Lightly oil a 13-by-9-inch baking dish and set aside.

Preheat oven to 375 degrees. Using a third of the tortilla chips, arrange a layer on the bottom of the prepared baking dish. Cover with 2 cups of the shredded cheese and 1 cup of the Salsa de Chile Pasilla. Make a second layer of chips and cover with the remaining 2 cups cheese and 1 cup sauce. Top with the remaining chips and pour the remaining Salsa de Chile Pasilla over the chips. Whisk milk and sour cream together and drizzle the mixture over the casserole. Cover with foil and bake about 45 minutes, or until the cheese is completely melted through. Serve warm. Serves 8.

### Variation

For Chilaquiles Verdes, replace the sauce with Salsa de Tomatillo and proceed as directed.

# MANCHAMANTELES
## Tablecloth Stainer

The brilliant red color of this dish is imparted by ancho chiles and tomatoes, and it will indeed stain your tablecloth, as the name implies. In the fall and winter months, it can also be made with sweet potatoes and dried fruit such as prunes. Chock-full of meat, vegetables, and savory fruit, it is well worth the risk of stained linens. Serve this dish with Arroz Blanco, Frijoles Refritos, and plenty of tortillas.

*¼ cup vegetable oil or lard*

*8 ancho chiles* ✿

*30 whole almonds*

*2 tablespoons sesame seeds, toasted*

*3 medium tomatoes, broiled* ✿

*4 cups chicken or pork broth*

*1 plantain, sliced and fried*

*1 small jícama, peeled and cubed*

*4 slices fresh pineapple, cubed*

*Sea salt to taste*

*2 cups cooked chicken, cut into 1- to 2-inch chunks*

*2 cups cooked pork, cut into 1- to 2-inch chunks*

In a heavy, 14-inch skillet or Dutch oven, heat oil over medium heat. Fry the chiles for about 10 seconds, or until they puff up; remove with a slotted spoon and set aside. Fry the almonds until golden; remove and set aside. Remove skillet from heat and reserve the oil for later. In a blender, combine chiles, almonds, sesame seeds, broiled tomatoes, and 1½ cups of the broth. Blend until smooth. Return skillet to medium heat and fry the chile mixture for about 5 minutes, stirring often, then add the remaining 2½ cups broth. Add the plantain, jícama, and pineapple and cook for about 25 minutes, stirring often. Add the chicken and pork and cook long enough to heat the meat through. Serves 8.

# CARNE GUISADA
## Stewed Beef

There are numerous versions of this tasty beef stew across the many states of Mexico. This particular rendition is from the northern state of Sonora and was passed down to Miguel from his beloved grandmother. In Arizona, where he grew up, it is often used as the hearty filling for burritos and tacos made with flour tortillas—the perfect portable meal.

*2 pounds round steak, cut into 1-inch chunks*

*4 tablespoons all-purpose flour*

*2 tablespoons vegetable oil*

*Half of a large white onion, sliced*

*2 medium tomatoes, chopped*

*½ cup chopped cilantro leaves*

*2 poblano chiles, roasted, peeled, seeded, and cut into ¼-inch strips, or 4 serrano chiles, chopped (or fewer for a milder dish)* ✿

*1 cup beef broth*

*1 teaspoon sea salt or to taste*

*Frijoles Refritos* ❖

*Arroz Mexicano* ❖

*Flour tortillas*

Dredge meat chunks in flour, coating well. In a heavy, 12-inch, deep-sided skillet or Dutch oven, heat the oil over medium heat and brown the meat thoroughly, stirring often, about 6 to 10 minutes. Add the onion, tomatoes, cilantro, and chiles and sauté for 3 to 4 minutes. Add beef broth, reduce heat to low, cover, and cook for 1 hour to 1 hour and 20 minutes, or until the beef is tender and the mixture has cooked down to a thick sauce. Add salt. Serve in individual serving bowls with Frijoles Refritos, Arroz Mexicano, and flour tortillas. Serves 6 to 8.

# BUDÍN DE ELOTE ❁
## Corn Pudding

This delicate soufflé-like dish, the Mexican counterpart to the spoon bread of the American South, is invariably the most popular dish on the Hacienda Sunday Brunch Buffet. It is especially good served with grilled meats, ham, or turkey in mole.

*2 pounds frozen corn kernels, thawed*

*Whole milk as needed (about 1 cup)*

*6 eggs, separated*

*½ cup sugar*

*6 tablespoons butter, softened*

*¾ cup all-purpose flour*

*1 teaspoon sea salt*

*1 teaspoon baking powder*

*1 cup (4 ounces) shredded Chihuahua, Monterey Jack, or cheddar cheese*

*1 poblano chile, roasted, peeled, seeded, and cut into ¼-inch strips* ✿

*Half of a red bell pepper, cut into strips*

Preheat oven to 350 degrees. Lightly grease a 13-by-9-inch baking dish and set aside. In a food processor fitted with a steel blade, puree the corn with only enough milk to make a smooth puree, not to exceed 1 cup. With the machine running, add egg yolks, one at a time, and process 30 seconds after each addition; next, add the sugar a little at a time and continue processing until mixture is lighter in color and sugar is dissolved, about 3 minutes. Add butter and process until smooth. Transfer to a large bowl. In a separate bowl, combine flour, salt, and baking powder; fold into corn mixture. Beat egg whites until soft peaks form and fold into corn mixture, alternating with the shredded cheese. Pour into the prepared baking dish and garnish with strips of chile and red bell pepper. Bake in preheated oven for 45 minutes, or until golden brown. Serve warm or at room temperature. Serves 8 or more.

**Francisco Toledo**

*Metates*, ca. 1992. Lithograph,
16 × 20 inches.

*Francisco Toledo is one of Mexico's greatest living artists, and his art can be rather astronomical in price. This piece, which I purchased in Austin from Galerie Ravel quite a few years ago, portrays the traditional implement for grinding corn, the metate, made of volcanic stone. Because of all the flying metates in this exquisite lithograph, I like to call it "Metates in the Sky"—sort of a Mexican rendition of "Ghost Riders in the Sky."*

*T.G.*

# CHIPOTLE POTATO GRATIN

Miguel devised this recipe to go with the wonderful Jamison Farms Lamb Chops on the dinner menu. He needed something creamy with a little bite to it, and this potato dish fit the bill. While Swiss or Jack cheese can be substituted for the Manchego, the Spanish cheese adds an important flavor element. The dish makes a great accompaniment to any grilled meat—beef or lamb. It also appears as a side dish on the Sunday buffet.

> 2 pounds Yukon gold or large red potatoes, peeled and thinly sliced
>
> 1 teaspoon sea salt
>
> 1¼ cups heavy cream
>
> 2 small garlic cloves, minced
>
> 2 to 3 chipotle chiles in adobo sauce, with 1 teaspoon sauce from the can ❀
>
> 2 cups (8 ounces) shredded Manchego cheese
>
> 2 tablespoons chopped chives

Preheat oven to 350 degrees. Butter a 13-by-9-inch glass or ceramic baking dish and set aside. Put potatoes and salt in a 3-quart saucepan and cover with water. Bring to a boil and boil potatoes for 6 minutes. Drain and set aside. In a blender, combine cream, garlic, and chiles; puree until smooth. Arrange half of the potatoes in the prepared baking dish. Pour half of the cream mixture evenly over the potatoes and sprinkle with half of the cheese. Repeat with the remaining potatoes, cream mixture, and cheese. Top with chopped chives. Cover with foil and bake for 30 minutes, or until the potatoes are tender. Uncover and bake an additional 30 minutes, or until the top is golden brown. Serve warm. Serves 6 to 8.

# CAMOTE Y PIÑA
## Sweet Potato Casserole with Pineapple

Sweet potatoes are not something most Americans associate with Mexican food, but they are very popular in Mexico and are often the basis for candies and other sweets. Guests at the Hacienda Sunday Brunch Buffet are always drawn to the brilliant orange color of this fragrant casserole studded with fresh pineapple. It's a worthy holiday side dish for both pork and poultry, and it could easily do double duty as a dessert.

> 6 large sweet potatoes (5½ to 6 pounds)
>
> ½ cup (1 stick) butter, softened
>
> ½ cup dark brown sugar
>
> 2 teaspoons ground cinnamon
>
> 1 teaspoon sea salt
>
> 1 small pineapple, cored, peeled, and cut into chunks

Lightly butter a 13-by-9-inch casserole dish and set aside. Line a baking sheet with foil and set aside. Preheat oven to 350 degrees. Prick the sweet potatoes all over with a fork and place them on the prepared baking sheet. Bake for about 1½ hours, or until they are soft. Remove from oven and set aside to cool. (Alternatively, make slits in the sweet potatoes and cook them three at a time in the microwave for about 15 minutes.) When the potatoes are cool enough to handle, peel them and put the pulp in a food processor. Add the softened butter, brown sugar, cinnamon, and salt; puree. Transfer to a bowl and fold in pineapple chunks. Pour the mixture into the prepared casserole dish. Bake for 30 minutes or until casserole is heated through. Serves 8.

# CHILES TOREADOS WITH ONIONS

## Sautéed Chiles with Onions

Chiles Toreados are usually served with hot corn tortillas for making tacos, or may be eaten as a topping for other foods. These can also be served with little tacos at cocktail time, with shots of tequila or mezcal. Eat with caution: a chile is less spicy at the tip end and much more spicy as you bite it near the stem end.

> ¾ cup olive oil (not virgin)
>
> 24 serrano chiles, stems left on
>
> 24 small knob onions—known in Mexico as cebollita de cambray (scallion or spring onion, with the "tail" still attached)
>
> Salt and pepper to taste

Use a heavy cast iron frying pan, if you have one. Over medium-high heat, sauté the chiles in a small amount of olive oil until they begin to blister slightly, about 5 minutes. Lower the heat and add the onions; sauté until they begin to soften and the outer layers are translucent. Add oil to the pan if necessary. Season with salt and pepper and remove from heat.

Arrange on a plate and serve with fresh, small, round Mexican limes, if desired.

# CEBOLLAS ROJAS EN ESCABECHE

## Pickled Red Onions

These bright red onion slices are a traditional garnish for Cochinita Pibil and Pescado Tikin Xik. They are nice to have on hand whenever you are serving grilled or barbecued meats. Miguel adds a fresh beet to the marinade mixture to increase the brilliance of the onions' color. Undrained, they will keep for several days in a sealed container in the refrigerator.

> 1 large red onion, thinly sliced
>
> 12 whole black peppercorns
>
> 3 garlic cloves, sliced
>
> 1 fresh beet, peeled and sliced
>
> 1 cup red wine vinegar

Combine ingredients in a nonreactive mixing bowl and set aside at room temperature for 1 to 2 hours. Remove beet slices and discard; drain onions and discard pickling liquid. Transfer onions to a serving dish and serve at room temperature. Serves 8 as a condiment.

# ESCABECHE DE VERDURAS
## Pickled Vegetables

This combination of pickled vegetables is a great addition to an appetizer platter or buffet and also complements grilled meat dishes. Like most pickled dishes, it tastes better after the vegetables have absorbed the pickling brine and the flavors are blended. Refrigerated, it keeps well for about two to three weeks.

*4 tablespoons olive oil*

*15 garlic cloves*

*6 fresh jalapeños, pierced with a fork* ✿

*2 dozen small boiler onions, peeled*

*4 carrots, peeled and cut into ¼-inch slices*

*1 quart water*

*2 medium red potatoes, cut into quarters*

*1 teaspoon sea salt*

Brine

*2 cups rice vinegar*

*1½ cups water*

*10 bay leaves*

*1 teaspoon ground cumin*

*1 teaspoon whole black peppercorns*

*1 teaspoon sea salt*

*3 sprigs marjoram*

*3 sprigs Mexican oregano*

*3 sprigs rosemary*

*1½ cups fresh green beans, with ends snapped*

*1½ cups small broccoli florets*

Heat olive oil in a heavy, 4-quart nonreactive saucepan over medium heat. Add garlic, jalapeños, onions, and carrots. Cook for about 10 minutes, or until the vegetables soften.

Add the brine ingredients and bring to a full boil. Reduce heat to medium and cook for 15 minutes.

In a separate 3-quart saucepan, bring water to a full boil. Add potatoes and cook at a brisk simmer for about 8 minutes. Drain potatoes and add to the vegetable-brine mixture. Add salt, adjusting seasonings as needed. Remove from heat and allow to cool to room temperature. Transfer to a nonreactive container and refrigerate 24 hours. Serves 12.

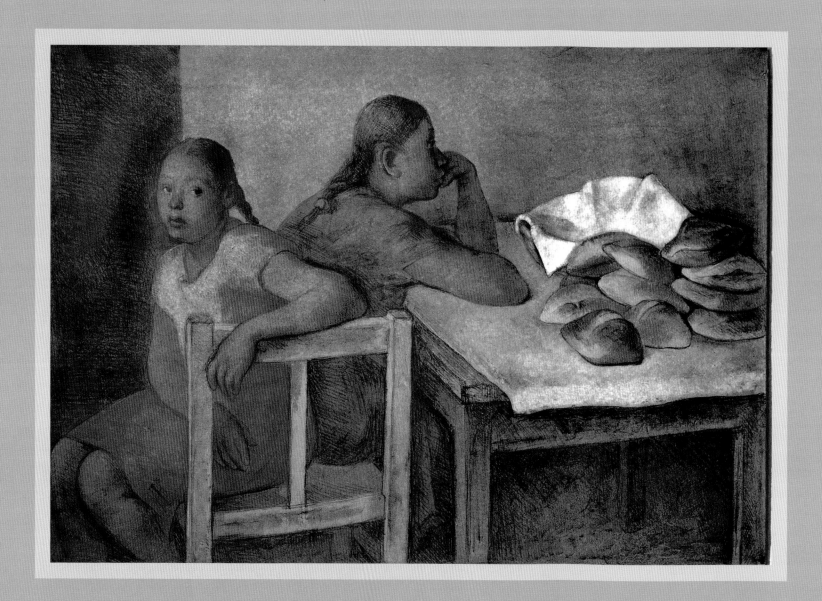

Francisco Zúñiga

*Panaderas*, 1995.
Lithograph, 22 × 32 inches.

*This group of lithographs by Francisco Zúñiga comprises some of the most important pieces in Fonda San Miguel's collection, so we usually display them together on a prominent wall. They were purchased some years ago from Dana Ravel at Galerie Ravel in Austin. Zúñiga was a painter, sculptor, and master printmaker and one of Latin America's most important artists. He is considered to be among the traditionalists, along with Tamayo, and is one of those artists whose works are known and collected by many people in Mexico.*

*T.G.*

Francisco Zúñiga

*La familia*, 1982.
Lithograph, 24 × 30½ inches.

Francisco Zúñiga

*La pescadora*, 1980.
Lithograph, 22 × 30 inches.

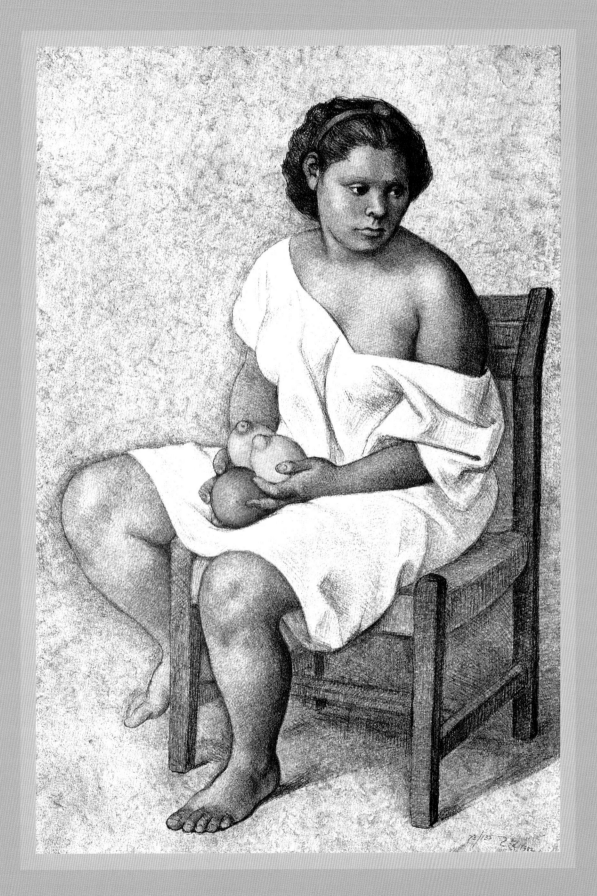

Francisco Zúñiga

*Niña con naranjas,* 1982.
Lithograph, 34 × 23 inches.

# Artist Juan Torres Calderón, Painter Of La boda

In August 2015, I invited Tom Gilliland to accompany me to an annual three-day Encuentro de Cocineras Tradicionales (festival of traditional cooks) in Morelia, the capital city of Mexico's state of Michoacán. Tom, brought to tears of joy by a talk given at the festival, was truly enraptured by his unique experiences there. In addition, he was astonished to discover that Susana Trilling, now owner of Oaxaca's Seasons of My Heart cooking school and a former employee in the Fonda San Miguel kitchen in the restaurant's early days, was also attending the festival. Their surprise reunion was a highlight of the weekend.

The festival, which was first held in 2002 in Uruapan, invites as many as sixty extraordinary indigenous home cooks from all over the state to participate in competitions and sales to the public of their families' most traditional dishes. Michoacán, which stretches from the Pacific Ocean to its land border with the central state of Mexico, delights in one of the most varied biospheres of Latin America. Michoacán's rich heritage of traditional food and the enormous number of specialties prepared by these indigenous women—along with a few men—attract approximately 35,000 hungry people to the yearly festivities.

In addition to spending food-filled days at the Encuentro, I offered Tom the opportunity to go with me on a tour of several rural towns in the countryside near Morelia. As we tooled along, Tom told me stories about some of his art-acquisition adventures in Mexico. *Se me prendió el foco*—a light bulb went on in my head: Maestro Juan Torres Calderón, one of Mexico's most prominent working artists and a close friend of mine, has for the last quarter-century made his home in the tiny rural town of Capula, Michoacán. His inspiration and images come most of-

ten from the history, landscapes, and people of the region. We were just a few kilometers from his home! "Want to see if he's in his studio, Tom?" And yes, Maestro Juan was at home and received us most graciously. We spent many hours with him, enjoying the typically Michoacán hospitality offered by the maestro and his wife, Velia Canals, an artist in her own right.

Maestro Torres says that he never made a conscious decision to become an artist; from an early age, he simply *was* an artist. At the tender age of ten, he went to Morelia's Escuela Popular de Bellas Artes (School of Fine Arts) "just to draw," and one of the teachers suggested that he enroll as a student at the school. "At that time there were no requirements that a student had to have completed elementary school, junior high, or high school—you just went and signed up. So I signed up. Like every other child in the world, I drew. The difference is, I never stopped drawing. One day, much to my amazement, I realized that there was a profession that would let me keep doing what I loved. And so I began my work as an artist."

One of Torres's profoundest influences at the beginning of his career was the legendary Michoacán artist Maestro Alfredo Zalce. Zalce (1908–2003) not only accepted the young Torres, he made him his primary assistant. "One way of learning art is, of course, imitating the teacher's work. It's a way of growing as an artist, and art is a job that requires growth or the artist stagnates.

"Many people think that the artist's life is bohemian—that it's all about sitting around cafés, waiting for inspiration to strike. A long time ago, someone gave me the advice that an artist has to work like the rest of the world. If it's at all possible, the artist needs to work at his

art eight hours a day. How can it be possible to wait for the muse, then to paint one painting a year, and still expect to evolve? If that's how he works, then every time the artist picks up a brush, he has to start from zero.

"So I prefer that people know me as someone who works in the arts. And that's what I do: I work at my job every day."

Entranced by Maestro Torres's home and studio, we spent happy hours looking at his extraordinary paintings. Tom ultimately decided to purchase *La boda* (67 ½ × 38 inches), which is now prominently displayed at Fonda San Miguel. Be sure to stop and enjoy it when you're dining at the restaurant. Maestro Torres knows his work is there, and next time I see him, I'll be sure to tell him you loved it.

—Cristina Potters

TORTILLAS Y PAN
Tortillas & Bread

Fresh handmade corn and flour tortillas are part of every meal at Fonda San Miguel. Although the type of tortilla is often a matter of individual preference, Miguel usually serves corn tortillas with chicken, fish, and pork dishes, and flour tortillas with beef dishes. The restaurant originally had no specific area for preparing tortillas, but during the extensive remodel in 1978 a tortilla station was added near the bar. Over the years, it has become quite an attraction for the public. Adults and children alike enjoy watching the tortilla makers gracefully slide sheets of masa onto the hot comales and artfully flip tortillas without burning their fingers. Fonda San Miguel is one of the few restaurants in Austin that offers fresh tortillas with every meal. (Once you've eaten a freshly made tortilla, it's difficult to reconcile yourself to the sad imitations at the grocery store.) Every week the restaurant goes through about five hundred pounds of fresh corn masa, delivered from a local tortilla factory. Tom and Miguel are working on a plan to import organic corn from Mexico so that organic masa can be prepared in the kitchen daily. Soon Fonda San Miguel will be the only Mexican restaurant in Texas (that we know of) to serve fresh organic corn tortillas. While tortillas are a daily ritual, other breads such as Rosca de Reyes and Pan de Muerto are important aspects of seasonal religious observances. Now that Pancho Álvarez is Fonda San Miguel's baker, he prepares those breads during the Epiphany season and for the restaurant's Day of the Dead altar.

# TORTILLAS DE MAÍZ
## Corn Tortillas

Corn tortillas are an essential food in all regions of Mexico. To prepare corn tortillas, you'll need masa harina (flour made from corn), as well as a tortilla press and a flat griddle or comal. La Paloma (or any available brand) packaged masa harina works fine. As a time-saver, you can look for a local tortilla factory or grocery store that sells fresh masa to the public.

> *2 cups masa harina plus additional as needed*
> *1¼ cups warm water*

In a large mixing bowl, mix the masa harina and water to make a soft dough. Add more masa harina if necessary to keep the dough from being sticky. Cover with plastic wrap and allow the dough to rest for 15 minutes. Divide dough into 15 equal portions, form balls of dough about the size of golf balls, and cover with plastic wrap or a dish towel so they do not dry out. Heat an ungreased griddle or comal over medium heat (make sure it does not get too hot or the tortillas will burn). Line the blades of the tortilla press with 2 sheets of plastic (a split 1-quart zip-sealing plastic bag works perfectly). Put a ball of masa between the sheets of plastic wrap and press the two blades together gently. Open the press and carefully peel off the top sheet of plastic. Lift the bottom sheet of plastic from the press; peel it away from the dough and slide the tortilla onto the hot griddle, being careful not to flip it over. Cook about 20 seconds on the first side. Using your fingers or a spatula, turn over and cook an additional 30 seconds on the second side. Turn over again and cook an additional 10 seconds on the first side. Keep warm tortillas in a basket lined with a napkin or dish towel while cooking the remaining tortillas. Makes 15 5- to 6-inch corn tortillas.

# TORTILLAS DE HARINA
## Flour Tortillas

Flour tortillas are much more typical of northern Mexico, a region of wheat and cattle, than of the central and southern parts of the country. La Paloma White Wings tortilla flour, available in most grocery stores, is a favorite with the Fonda San Miguel tortilla makers. Your regular rolling pin will work fine for flour tortillas.

> *4 cups tortilla flour*
> *2 teaspoons sea salt*
> *½ cup Crisco shortening or lard*
> *1 cup lukewarm water*

In a large mixing bowl, sift together flour and salt. Add shortening and mix well with your hands until mixture is crumbly. Add warm water and mix to form a soft dough. Turn dough out onto a lightly floured board and knead for about 3 minutes. Divide dough into 12 equal portions and form into balls. Rub hands with a little shortening and roll each ball gently to coat with shortening. Cover with a dish towel and allow to rest for about 15 minutes. On a lightly floured surface, roll each ball into a circle about 8 inches in diameter. Heat an ungreased griddle or comal over medium heat. Cook tortilla on one side about 30 to 45 seconds, or until bubbles begin to appear and the edges are golden. Using your fingers or a spatula, turn over and cook on the other side an additional 45 seconds to 1 minute. Keep warm tortillas in a basket lined with a napkin or dish towel while cooking the remaining tortillas. Makes 12 8-inch tortillas.

# BOLILLOS
## Crusty Bread Rolls

These oval bread rolls hark back to the days of the French occupation and its culinary influence in Mexico. Bolillos are often hollowed out and filled with refried beans, picadillo, or Carne Guisada for a hearty portable meal. They are also the basis for Mexican sandwiches called tortas. Like any good French bread roll, they make a wonderful addition to a dinner party when served warm with sweet butter. The recipe here is adapted from a version published in *Cocina de la Familia,* written by Marilyn Tausend with Miguel Ravago.

> *2½ cups warm water*
> *1 tablespoon sugar*
> *2 ½-ounce packages active dry yeast*
> *½ cup olive oil or lard*
> *1 tablespoon plus 1 teaspoon sea salt*
> *5 cups all-purpose flour*
> *⅓ cup masa harina*
> *⅓ cup white cornmeal*

Place ½ cup of the warm water in a small bowl. (Test a drop on the inside of your wrist; it should be comfortably warm.) Add sugar and yeast, stir, and set aside until yeast has dissolved and mixture is foamy and bubbly, about 5 minutes.

In a large bowl, mix together 1½ cups of the warm water, oil, 1 tablespoon of the salt, 2 cups of the flour, and the proofed yeast mixture. Stir well with a wooden spoon to make a creamy batter. Add about 2½ cups of the flour, a little at a time, along with the masa harina and cornmeal. Continue stirring until the dough pulls away from the sides of the bowl and is rather firm. If dough is too stiff, add more water as needed, 1 tablespoon at a time.

Turn out the dough onto a lightly floured surface and knead, adding more flour if the dough becomes sticky. Continue to knead until dough is firm, resilient, and satiny smooth, about 4 minutes. Place dough in a large, lightly oiled bowl, turning to coat all surfaces. Cover with plastic wrap or a dish towel and allow to rise in a warm place for 1 hour, or until doubled in bulk.

Turn out the dough onto the lightly floured surface and knead for 2 minutes. Divide dough into 4 equal portions. Keeping remaining portions covered, divide a dough portion into 4 rolls. Form each roll into a flat oval, pinching the ends to form a spindle shape. Repeat with the remaining portions.

Place rolls on ungreased baking sheets, cover, and let rise in a warm place until doubled in bulk, about 30 minutes. Meanwhile, preheat oven to 375 degrees.

Mix the remaining ¼ cup water with the 1 teaspoon salt and lightly brush the top of the rolls. Pinch ends again. Using a sharp, thin-bladed knife, cut a shallow diagonal slit in the top of each roll. Bake rolls in preheated oven for 20 to 30 minutes, lowering heat to 350 degrees if they brown too quickly. When the rolls are a pale golden color and sound hollow when tapped, remove from the oven and cool on a rack. Makes 16 rolls.

# ROSCA DE REYES
## Three Kings' Cake

This sweet yeast bread is shaped in a ring and studded with candied fruits to resemble a crown. It is served on January 6 to celebrate the arrival of the Three Kings in Bethlehem. Mexican bakeries in Austin often prepare it during the Christmas season. Candied fruits such as pineapple, cherries, and citron are usually available in grocery stores at that time of year. The baker hides a tiny china baby doll, bean, or penny in the dough, and tradition holds that the person who finds the prize is king for that party and the host of the next celebration. This not-too-sweet bread is delicious served with Chocolate a la Mexicana.

2 ½-ounce packages dry active yeast

¼ cup warm water

4 cups all-purpose flour

2 eggs, beaten

¾ cup sugar

¼ teaspoon sea salt

6 egg yolks, beaten

2 tablespoons water

1 tablespoon grated orange zest

1 tablespoon grated lemon zest

1 cup butter, softened

2 cups chopped candied fruit plus additional for garnish

½ cup chopped pecans or walnuts plus additional for garnish

½ cup raisins

2 china baby dolls, or substitute large beans or clean pennies

1 egg, beaten lightly with 1 tablespoon water

## Topping

2 cups confectioners' sugar or powdered sugar

⅓ cup orange juice

Reserved candied fruit and nuts (about ¼ cup each)

In a medium mixing bowl, dissolve yeast in the warm water and add about 1 cup of the flour, or enough to form a soft dough. Cover with a dish towel and set aside to rise in a warm, draft-free spot until doubled in bulk, about 1 hour. Put the remaining 3 cups flour in a second bowl, make a well in the center, and put the 2 eggs, sugar, and salt in the well. Work together with your hands. Add the egg yolks, water, orange zest, and lemon zest. Add the yeast mixture and butter and mix. Turn out onto a lightly floured surface and knead until dough is smooth and elastic, about 5 to 8 minutes. Place dough in a lightly oiled bowl, cover with a towel, and set aside to rise in a draft-free spot until doubled in bulk, about 1 hour. Grease a baking sheet or line with parchment paper and set aside.

When dough has doubled in bulk, knead in the candied fruit, nuts, and raisins. Divide dough into two portions. Roll out each portion into a rectangle approximately 8 by 12 inches. Roll up the dough from the long side as you would a jelly roll, hiding a baby doll in the loaf. Repeat with the remaining portion. Join the ends to make ring-shaped loaves or "crowns." Place on the prepared baking sheet, cover with a dish towel, and let rise for about 1 hour.

Preheat oven to 375 degrees. Brush loaves lightly with egg wash and bake in preheated oven for about 30 minutes, or until loaves sound hollow when tapped. Remove from baking sheet and cool on wire racks.

To prepare the topping, whisk together the powdered sugar and orange juice to make a smooth glaze. Drizzle over the warm loaves and sprinkle with the reserved candied fruit and nuts. Makes 2 loaves.

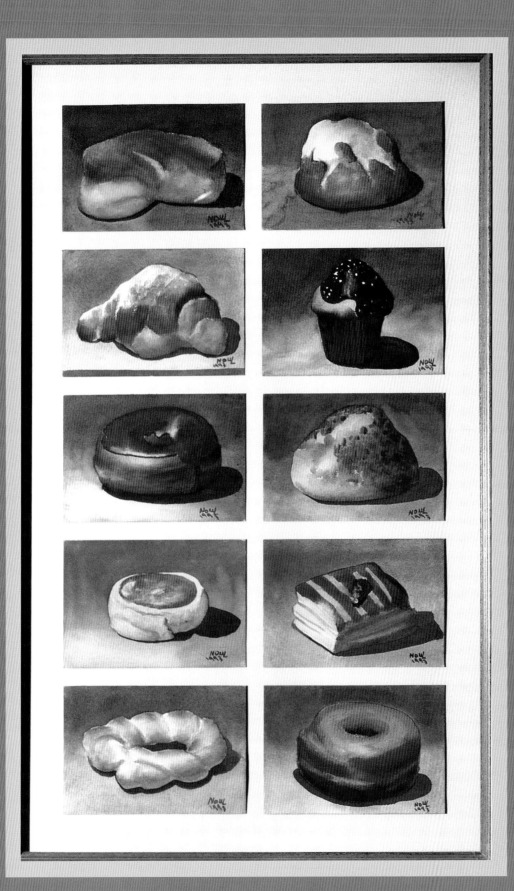

## Noel

Ten untitled watercolors, ca. 1993, each 8 × 5½ inches.

*I bought these watercolors of Mexican breads and pastries in Mexico City and then had them all framed together.*

*T.G.*

In Mexico, November 1 is a day when ancient Mexican folk religions and Catholic traditions collide in elaborate celebrations of *El Día de los Muertos*, the Day of the Dead. Villagers honor their dead by cleaning cemeteries and building altars, or *ofrendas*, decked with fragrant incense, bright marigolds, sugar skulls, and samples of the departed loved one's favorite foods and beverages. Once the festivities have ended, families gather and eat this yeast bread with *Café de Olla* or *Chocolate a la Mexicana*.

# PAN DE MUERTO
## Bread for Day of the Dead

*2 juice oranges (you will use both skin and juice)*

*½ cup water*

*3½ cups all-purpose white flour*

*½ cup granulated sugar*

*2 tablespoons fast-acting granular yeast*

*½ cup butter*

*3 whole eggs*

*5 egg yolks*

*⅓ cup vegetable shortening*

*1 tablespoon orange flavoring*

*2 teaspoons anise extract*

*¼ teaspoon salt*

*Additional flour for kneading*

*2 tablespoons butter for melting*

*Granulated sugar for sprinkling on the bread*

Wash the oranges well. Using a very fine grater or a microplane, grate the outer skin of each orange and reserve. Juice the oranges and reserve the juice. You should have ½ cup orange juice; if you don't have quite enough, add water to bring it to ½ cup. Set aside.

Heat the ½ cup water but do not allow it to boil. It should feel warm when you put a finger into the water, but it should not burn. Combine 2 tablespoons of the flour with 2 teaspoons of the granulated sugar. Add the yeast and the water and stir gently with a teaspoon until the yeast begins to release tiny bubbles on the surface of the water.

In a large bowl, place the rest of the flour and granulated sugar. Make a well in the center of these ingredients and add the butter, the eggs, and the additional yolks, the vegetable shortening, the orange rind, and the orange juice. Stir with a spoon or a wooden spatula until the ingredients are well mixed. Add the orange flavoring, the anise extract, and the yeast mixture and mix again.

Once all the ingredients are incorporated, start kneading with your hands, first within the bowl and, once the dough has come together, on a floured board. Knead for approximately 15 minutes, until the dough no longer sticks. You will know that it is ready when you can stretch it approximately one foot without it breaking.

Form a single ball of dough and place it in a glass or metal bowl. Cover it with a thin damp towel and put the bowl in a warm spot where no air blows on it. Allow the dough to rest until it doubles in size, between 30 to 60 minutes.

Line two cookie sheets with parchment paper. Move one of the racks of your oven to the top third and the other rack to the bottom third.

Once doubled in size, take the dough from the bowl and knead it again for a few minutes, adding the salt and making sure it is well incorporated into the dough.

Cut the dough into five equal parts. Four parts will be the loaves of bread and the fifth will be used to make the traditional decorative "bones" for the top of each loaf. Make four spheres and place them on the cookie sheets, two per sheet. Leave enough space between the spheres so that they will not touch during baking.

Divide the fifth part of the dough into four sections. With each of the sections, you will make two 4-inch-long strips of dough and one small round ball. Roll the strips with your fingers so that the ends are slightly thinner than the center sections. Place the strips of rolled dough across the tops of the bread so that two strips cross one another. Press lightly so that the strips stick to the bread. Place one of the small balls of dough on top of the bread where the dough strips cross.

Using a brush dipped in water, slightly dampen the entire surface of each bread and its "bones." This prevents the surface of the bread from drying out in the oven.

Allow the breads to rest in a warm place for approximately 45 minutes or until doubled in size.

Preheat the oven to 350 degrees. Bake, one sheet on each oven rack, for 20 to 25 minutes, or until they are golden brown all over.

Remove the bread from the oven and place the cookie sheets on wire racks.

Melt two tablespoons of butter and brush the butter over the entire surface (including the "bones") of the warm bread. Immediately sprinkle each loaf with a liberal amount of granulated sugar.

Allow the loaves to cool completely. If you are not going to eat them immediately, wrap the breads in plastic wrap so that they stay soft. Makes 4 medium-sized loaves.

### Arnulfo Mendoza

Untitled, circa 1990. Vegetable and insect dyes, silk, 67 × 87 inches.

*A master rug weaver and painter from Oaxaca, Arnulfo Mendoza created this magnificent tapestry, which uses insect and vegetable dyes with interwoven silk. A friend of Fonda San Miguel for many years until his untimely death in 2014, Arnulfo created unique and diverse art that has become a treasured part of our collection.*

*T.G.*

Pablo Casovas

*Flooded Cathedral*, 2011. 58 × 62 inches.

*I purchased this very unusual "flooded cathedral" by Spanish artist Casovas at Art Madrid Exposition.*

T.G.

# POSTRES
## Desserts

As Fonda San Miguel's first pastry chef, Virginia was the first to admit ignorance of traditional Mexican sweets when she initially came to the restaurant. A native Texan, she grew up thinking that a Mexican meal was followed by a frosty dish of rainbow sherbet or a sugary pecan praline. This was one of many Tex-Mex traditions that Miguel was determined to break! He didn't issue many strict dessert guidelines other than that. Virginia was a quick study, however, and soon created a creamy chocolate pie spiked with Kahlua as well as a festive tart topped with mangoes. Traditional Mexican desserts proved to be a harder sell. There were mangoes flamed in tequila served over ice cream from a Diana Kennedy recipe, and the family heirloom flan shared by a generous customer that became a signature dish. But the truth is, the most popular dessert in the early days of the restaurant was a deep-dish sour cream apple pie, created by former sous chef Susana Trilling. Mexican-inspired dishes eventually filled out the menu, and soon customers were enjoying delicate cajeta crepes and exquisite tropical sorbets. The current baker, Pancho Álvarez of Zacatecas, provides the most authentic Mexican desserts ever to grace a Fonda San Miguel table. The Hacienda Sunday Brunch Buffet has proven to be the best venue for introducing those items to the dining public. Pancho carefully prepares the Capirotada, Natilla, and Arroz con Leche handed down from Miguel's grandmother. Then he turns his hand to his own version of the popular Tres Leches cake and a delightful assortment of Mexican cookies—and the customers love them.

# FLAN ALMENDRADO
## Almond Flan

Flan is one of the most traditional desserts in the entire Hispanic-influenced world—from Spain and Portugal to Cuba and Puerto Rico, all the way to Mexico and Central and South America. It comes in a variety of flavors and textures, depending on the local tastes and agricultural products of each region. When Fonda San Miguel opened in 1975, few, if any, Mexican restaurants in Texas offered flan as a dessert option. In the early days of the restaurant, a loyal customer named Ana María generously shared her family's heirloom recipe from the Mexican state of Guanajuato, and it has been a customer favorite ever since. It's very dense and creamy, balanced by a crunchy almond crust on the bottom.

*¾ cup sugar*

*⅔ cup blanched, slivered almonds*

*1½ 14-ounce cans Eagle Brand sweetened condensed milk*

*1 cup whole milk*

*3 whole eggs*

*3 egg yolks*

*1 teaspoon Mexican vanilla extract* ✿

Preheat the oven to 350 degrees. Place oven rack in middle position. Put sugar in a round 9-by-3-inch cake pan. Using a heavy oven mitt or tongs, place the pan directly over medium heat to caramelize the sugar. Heat until the sugar liquefies, about 3 to 5 minutes, stirring occasionally with a wooden spoon. *Do not touch the melted sugar*—it will cause serious burns. When the hot liquid in the pan is a golden brown color, remove from heat and set aside on a rack to cool and harden.

In a blender, combine the almonds, condensed milk, whole milk, eggs, yolks, and vanilla. Process on medium speed until well blended. Pour custard mixture over the prepared caramel. Place the cake pan in a larger, deeper pan and pour about an inch of hot water around the cake pan to make a water bath. Cover the flan loosely with a foil tent and place the larger pan on the middle rack of the preheated oven. Bake for 1 hour and 15 minutes, or until flan is set in the center (it will no longer jiggle). Remove from the oven and cool on a rack at room temperature. Refrigerate until thoroughly chilled, at least 1 hour.

To serve, run a knife or thin spatula around the edge of the flan to release it from the sides of the pan. Place a 10-inch (or larger) serving platter on top of the pan. Turn the platter over and gently remove the cake pan, leaving flan on the serving platter. Using a flexible spatula, scrape up as much of the caramel as possible from the bottom of the pan and pour over the flan. Cut into triangular wedges and serve. Makes 8 to 12 slices.

Arnulfo Mendoza

*Manzanero,* ca. 1992.
Oil on gouache, 18 × 24 inches.

*This absolutely gorgeous watercolor by Arnulfo Mendoza shows many heart-shaped apples coming out of a tree as a half-animal, half-human figure looks on. Multi-talented Arnulfo, from Teotitlan in the state of Oaxaca, was also a renowned weaver.*

*T.G.*

# APPLE PIE SAN MIGUEL

While apple pie is by no means a Mexican dessert, this remarkable all-American version was the hands-down favorite dessert at Fonda San Miguel for several years. In the late 1970s, a talented young chef named Susana Trilling worked at Fonda San Miguel as a sous chef presenting a lunch menu with an international flair. She brought the recipe with her from Philadelphia to Austin, where the pie became an instant hit at the restaurant. Since the early 1990s, Susana has operated Seasons of My Heart Cooking School outside Oaxaca, where she writes cookbooks and trains chefs and avocational cooks from all over the world. Although Fonda San Miguel hasn't served this pie in many years, longtime customers still request it from time to time. It's the best apple pie we've ever tasted and makes a great addition to any holiday feast.

## Cinnamon Pie Crust

*1½ cups all-purpose flour*

*½ teaspoon sea salt*

*3 tablespoons sugar*

*2 teaspoons ground cinnamon*

*½ cup (1 stick) cold unsalted butter, cut into chunks*

*Ice-cold apple juice to bind*

## Apple–Sour Cream Filling

*1¼ cups sour cream*

*¾ cup sugar*

*½ teaspoon sea salt*

*3 tablespoons all-purpose flour*

*1 egg*

*1 teaspoon Mexican vanilla extract* ✿

*6 Granny Smith apples*

## Brown Sugar and Walnut Topping

*½ cup brown sugar*

*½ cup white sugar*

*1 cup all-purpose flour*

*1 teaspoon ground cinnamon*

*1 teaspoon sea salt*

*1 cup toasted walnuts, coarsely chopped*

*6 tablespoons unsalted butter, melted*

To make the crust, combine flour, salt, sugar, and cinnamon in a mixing bowl. Using a stand mixer with a paddle attachment or a pastry cutter, cut in the butter until the mixture resembles coarse crumbs, about 2 to 3 minutes. Add apple juice sparingly and mix 1 to 2 minutes, or until dough comes together in a ball. Form dough into a flat disk, wrap in plastic wrap, and refrigerate at least 1 hour. On a lightly floured board, roll dough out into an 11- or 12-inch circle. Fold dough in half, then in quarters, and place in a 10-inch, deep-dish pie pan. Carefully unfold and fit dough in bottom and against sides of pan. Make a rolled border around the edge with overhanging dough and crimp in a decorative pattern. Refrigerate pie shell at least 1 hour or freeze for later use.

Meanwhile, make the filling. Preheat oven to 400 degrees. Put sour cream in a 3-quart mixing bowl. In a separate bowl, combine sugar, salt, and flour; whisk into sour cream. Whisk in egg and vanilla. Peel, core, and slice the apples, immersing them in the sour cream mixture as you work. (The acid in the sour cream will keep the apples from turning brown.) Stir to mix well. Fill the chilled pie shell with the apple mixture, mounding it higher in the center. Place the pie on a cookie sheet on the middle rack of the preheated oven. Bake for 10 minutes, lower heat to 350 degrees, and bake an additional 40 minutes.

While the pie is baking, make the topping. Combine dry ingredients in a mixing bowl. Add melted butter, a couple of tablespoons at a time, and mix with your hands until mixture holds together but is not greasy. Set aside.

When pie is done, remove from oven and carefully sprinkle with the topping mixture, covering the apple filling evenly all over the top of the pie. Return to oven and bake an additional 10 minutes. Remove from oven and cool on a rack. Chill before serving. Serves 8 to 12.

*NOTE:* Although this pie cuts more easily when chilled, it is wonderful if served while still warm. It can also be frozen successfully.

## Danny Brennan

*Postres rosados,* 1978.
Oil on canvas, 31½ × 47½ inches.

This painting of two girls and four pink cakes is a work that everyone loves for its vibrant colors. It's really one of my favorite pieces, and it's on the front of one of the Fonda San Miguel matchboxes. We probably have seven or eight paintings by Danny Brennan in our collection—it may be one of the biggest Brennan collections around. One day I'll hang them all together in one room and have a show; the effect would be quite dramatic! Another of his paintings in our collection is a big one titled The French Park, which is the name of an actual park in San Miguel de Allende. But the painting shows a girl sitting beside a fountain and playing a saxophone for animals that aren't found in the park, so the artist obviously had quite an imagination. I purchased several of Danny's paintings by walking out to his studio, about a mile from San Miguel de Allende. I found him hard at work, and he barely acknowledged me. I said hello, he said hi, and that was about it. I looked around and saw some paintings that I liked. When I asked how much, he said, "I don't know . . . whatever you say." That's an awkward predicament, when an artist tells you to put a price on his work. Even so, I walked away from his studio with three paintings under my arm, unframed. Not long after this, Danny was "discovered" by Nelson Rockefeller's art curators, and Danny's paintings suddenly became worth a lot more money. But that was fine with me, because I had already beaten Rockefeller to the punch.

*T.G.*

# SPICED RUM APPLES

Although this is not a particularly Mexican recipe, it works extremely well as a topping for Fonda San Miguel's traditional Arroz con Leche (Rice Pudding). (See separate recipe.)

*¼ cup unsalted butter*

*4 tart, crisp apples, peeled and cut into 8 wedges each*

*½ teaspoon ground mixed spice*

*3 tablespoons dark rum*

*2 tablespoons Mexican table cream (or crème fraiche)*

In a large frying pan, melt half the butter and sizzle the apple wedges for 10 minutes, turning them now and then, until they are golden and softened. Transfer the apples and butter to a plate.

Add the remaining butter to the pan, then the sugar and the spices. Once the butter has melted, add the rum. Be careful, it may splatter a bit. Then stir in the cream to make a silky sauce. Return the apples to the pan and serve with Arroz con Leche (Rice Pudding). Serves 8.

# TROPICAL TART

A hot young magazine called *Texas Monthly* held its fifth anniversary party at Fonda San Miguel in 1978. As the pastry chef, Virginia designed this festive tart especially for the big celebration (but publisher Mike Levy still insisted on having a slice of his favorite: Coffee-Toffee Pie). The component parts of the tart can be made in advance to be assembled when it's time for dessert. The tart makes a dramatic and colorful presentation at parties. It's best when eaten on the same day it's made.

### Crust

*1 cup toasted pecans, chopped*

*1 cup all-purpose flour*

*⅓ cup dark brown sugar*

*½ teaspoon ground cinnamon*

*½ teaspoon sea salt*

*6 tablespoons cold butter, cut into chunks*

*1 egg*

### Filling

*1 cup heavy cream*

*4 ounces cream cheese, softened*

*3 tablespoons powdered sugar*

*1 teaspoon Mexican vanilla extract or dark rum ✽*

### Topping

*2 tablespoons dark rum*

*2 tablespoons boiling water*

*¾ cup raisins*

*2 ripe mangoes, peeled and cored, or 1 can mangoes, drained and sliced ✽*

*¾ cup toasted pecans, chopped*

*1 6-ounce jar pineapple preserves*

Prepare the crust. Preheat oven to 350 degrees. Combine all crust ingredients in the bowl of a food processor and pulse until dough comes together in large clumps. Press dough into the bottom and against the sides of an 11-inch tart pan with a removable bottom. Prick all over with a fork and bake 12 to 15 minutes in preheated oven, or until the crust is golden brown and fragrant. Set aside on a rack to cool. (The cooled tart shell can be wrapped in the pan and frozen for later use.)

Meanwhile, prepare the filling. In a chilled bowl with chilled beaters, beat the cream until stiff peaks form; cover tightly and refrigerate. In another mixing bowl, beat the cream cheese until it is light and fluffy, add the sugar and vanilla, and beat until smooth. Using a rubber spatula, gently fold the chilled whipped cream into the cream cheese mixture until it is well mixed. Spread the filling in the cooled tart shell and refrigerate.

To make the topping, combine rum and boiling water in a small bowl and add raisins. Allow to steep for about 5 minutes while you prepare the mangoes. Slice mango halves lengthwise in long, thin strips and set aside on paper towels. Combine raisins and their liquid, pecans, and preserves in a small, nonreactive saucepan. Simmer over medium heat for about 5 minutes, stirring often, or until liquid has reduced and mixture is shiny. Set aside to cool.

To assemble the tart, arrange mango slices in the chilled tart shell by fanning them in a circle, starting about ¼ inch inside the outer rim of the crust, covering all the filling. Using a spoon, put a ring of the topping mixture around the outside rim of the tart, just inside the crust, and a smaller ring in the center. Reserve any leftover topping for another use. (It's good on ice cream.) Chill until ready to serve. Remove tart by holding the tart tin on an outstretched palm and gently easing the side down. Slice into wedges. Serves 10 to 12.

*NOTE:* For a lighter flavor, the topping can be made with golden raisins (pictured). You can also vary the presentation by spooning the topping over the center of the tart or putting a dollop on each slice.

# CREPAS DE CAJETA
## Crepes with Caramelized Goat's Milk Sauce

This elegant dessert reflects the French culinary influence in Mexican cuisine. Delicate French crepes are sauced with *cajeta*, a traditional Mexican caramel made of goat's milk. Movie director Robert Rodriguez and his wife Elizabeth once invited an *Entertainment Weekly* journalist to the restaurant as their guest and ordered Crepas de Cajeta for dessert. He took one bite, inhaled deeply with his eyes closed, and said, "And Jesus wept"—with the deep conviction of a new convert. The crepes make a perfect dinner party dessert because they can be assembled at the last minute from components prepared in advance. They are also delicious with various flavors of ice cream. Store any extra sauce covered in the refrigerator and gently reheat as a topping for ice cream.

> 1¼ cups all-purpose flour
> 3 large eggs, lightly beaten
> ⅔ cup milk, plus additional as needed
> ⅔ cup water
> 2 tablespoons unsalted butter, melted and cooled
> 2 teaspoons sea salt
> Safflower oil
> Ice cream
> 2 cups sliced almonds (skins on), toasted

### Goat's Milk Sauce

> ½ cup (1 stick) butter
> ¼ cup Kahlua coffee liqueur
> ¼ cup sour cream
> 1 10.9-ounce jar Coronado cajeta ✿

Combine flour, eggs, milk, water, butter, and salt in a blender and mix until smooth. Add a little more milk if necessary (the batter should be thin). Cover with plastic wrap and set aside to rest for 30 minutes.

Line a plate with waxed paper or baker's parchment and set aside. Warm a 6-inch nonstick crepe pan over medium-high heat and brush with a little oil. Do not let it smoke. Ladle about 3 tablespoons of batter (a 1½-ounce ladle works well) into the hot pan and swirl the batter around to cover the bottom of the pan. Once bubbles begin to form on the surface, use a flexible spatula to lift up the edges of the crepe. Flip over and cook on the second side for an additional 45 seconds. Remove from heat, transfer to the prepared plate, and cover with a layer of waxed paper. Repeat the process until all crepe batter is used, alternating crepes with layers of paper. (Leftover crepes can be wrapped well and frozen.)

Prepare the Goat's Milk Sauce. Combine butter, liqueur, sour cream, and *cajeta* in a heavy, 2-quart nonreactive saucepan over medium heat and stir until the butter melts. Do not boil. Remove from heat and keep warm.

To assemble, fold crepes in quarters and place 2 crepes on each of 6 dessert plates. Pour about ¼ cup of the warm sauce over each pair of crepes and top with a scoop of ice cream. Sprinkle with toasted almonds. Serves 6.

# PASTEL DE TRES LECHES
## Three-Milk Cake

No one seems to know exactly where this rich, moist cake originated. It is claimed by many regions in Mexico, Central America, and the Caribbean. This particular recipe was given to Miguel by Bobby and Laura Shapiro while he was the executive chef at one of their Zócalo restaurants in New York. He once prepared it for 350 guests at a Cinco de Mayo celebration at the Mexican consulate in New York City, making all the local papers. The cake is a regular feature on the dessert table at the Hacienda Sunday Brunch Buffet.

*1½ cups all-purpose flour*

*1 teaspoon baking powder*

*½ teaspoon sea salt*

*6 eggs*

*1 cup sugar*

*¼ cup water*

*3 teaspoons Mexican vanilla extract* ✽

*1 14-ounce can sweetened condensed milk*

*1 13-ounce can evaporated milk*

*3 cups heavy cream*

*Fresh mangoes, strawberries, peaches, or other fresh fruit, sliced*

Spray the bottom and sides of a 9-by-3-inch springform pan with vegetable cooking spray and set aside. Preheat oven to 350 degrees. Sift together flour, baking powder, and salt; set aside. Combine eggs and sugar in the bowl of a stand mixer and beat on high speed until doubled in volume, about 5 minutes. Reduce speed to low; add the water and 1 teaspoon of the vanilla. Mix well. On very low speed or by hand using a long spatula, gently fold dry ingredients into the batter. Pour batter into the prepared pan and bake for 35 to 40 minutes, or until the cake is firm on top and has pulled away from the sides of the pan. Remove from oven and place pan on a rack to cool for 10 to 15 minutes. Turn the cake out on a serving platter, place a cake plate over the cake, and turn it right side up. Set aside to continue cooling.

While the cake is cooling, whisk together the sweetened condensed milk, the evaporated milk, the remaining 2 teaspoons vanilla, and 1 cup of the heavy cream; set aside. Using a serrated knife, gently slice off the top skin of the cake and discard. Prick the cake all over with a long toothpick. (This will allow the cake to soak up the milk mixture.) Pour milk mixture over the cake in several batches, allowing it to soak in as much as possible each time. Refrigerate.

When ready to serve, pour the remaining 2 cups heavy cream into a chilled bowl and beat with chilled beaters until stiff peaks form. Pipe or spread the whipped cream on the top and sides of the cake and garnish with fresh fruit slices. Serves 8 to 12.

# ARROZ CON LECHE
## Rice Pudding

Rice pudding is a well-established comfort food in many cultures around the globe. Like flan, it is one of the many European-style sweets that were introduced into the Mexican culinary lexicon by Spanish Catholic nuns. Miguel's recipe is laborious, but the result is rich and creamy, studded with plump raisins. It relies on aromatic Mexican vanilla beans and the more subtle Mexican cinnamon for a touch of spice. Arroz con Leche has a very loyal following among regular patrons of the Hacienda Sunday Brunch Buffet.

*2½ quarts water*

*1 cup raw long-grain white rice*

*1 quart whole milk*

*1 12-ounce can evaporated milk*

*1 cup sugar*

*1 Mexican vanilla bean, split lengthwise* ✽

*1 3-inch Mexican cinnamon stick* ✽

*½ cup raisins*

*Ground cinnamon for garnish*

Bring 1 quart of the water to a boil in a medium saucepan. Remove from heat and add rice; let stand for 20 minutes. Drain and rinse well. In another saucepan, bring the remaining 1½ quarts water to a boil and add rice. Boil uncovered until rice is tender, about 8 to 10 minutes. Do not overcook. Drain and set aside.

Scald whole milk in a 4-quart saucepan; add evaporated milk, sugar, vanilla bean, and cinnamon stick. Cook over medium heat for 45 minutes, stirring regularly, until mixture reduces somewhat and begins to turn a light golden color. Remove vanilla bean and cinnamon stick. Add rice and raisins and cook for another 25 minutes over medium to medium-low heat, stirring regularly, until pudding thickens. Remove from heat, stirring occasionally until pudding cools. Transfer to a serving platter and sprinkle with ground cinnamon. Serve chilled or at room temperature. Serves 6 to 8.

# CAPIROTADA MEXICAN
## Bread Pudding

Though *capirotada* is traditionally served during the Lenten season, you'll find various versions of it around Mexico during most times of the year. It is a multiethnic dish relying on French bread, cheddar cheese, tropical fruits, and Mexican seasonings. Don't be alarmed by the savory ingredients—the finished product is quite delicious. This recipe comes from Miguel's grandmother.

*1 1-pound loaf French bread, sliced and lightly toasted*

*3 cups sliced bananas*

*4 tablespoons ground cinnamon*

*½ cup fresh cilantro, chopped*

*1 cup (4 ounces) grated cheddar cheese*

*1 cup dark raisins*

*½ cup chopped green onions, including green tops*

*1 cup dry-roasted peanuts*

*1 cup candied pineapple, chopped*

*6 eggs*

*2 cups heavy cream*

*Fresh mint sprigs for garnish*

### Syrup

*4 cups water*

*2 8-ounce cones piloncillo, grated* ✽

*1 cup light brown sugar*

*2 tablespoons anise seeds*

*1 6-inch Mexican cinnamon stick* ✽

*¼ cup Mexican vanilla extract* ✽

*1 cup (2 sticks) butter*

Grease a 13-by-9-inch baking dish and set aside. Cut or tear the toasted bread into bite-size pieces and put in a large, non-reactive mixing bowl. Add bananas, ground cinnamon, cilantro, cheese, raisins, green onions, peanuts, and pineapple; toss together with your hands or two large spoons. In a separate bowl, whisk the eggs together lightly and add to the bread mixture, tossing gently. Set aside.

To prepare the syrup, combine all ingredients in a heavy, 2-quart saucepan. Bring to a boil over medium-high heat, reduce heat to low, and simmer for about 20 minutes.

Preheat oven to 350 degrees. Transfer bread mixture to the prepared baking pan and strain the hot syrup over the bread mixture. Cover with foil and bake for 1 hour. Remove from oven and cool on a rack for a few minutes.

In a chilled bowl with chilled beaters, beat the cream until stiff peaks form. Spoon warm pudding into individual serving bowls; top each serving with a generous dollop of whipped cream and a sprig of fresh mint. Serves 12 to 16.

# CAJETA
## Caramelized Goat's Milk

This caramelized goat's-milk candy gets its name from the little boxes *(cajetas)* in which it was originally sold on the streets in Mexico. These days it is possible to purchase commercial brands, such as Coronado, but there is also a certain amount of satisfaction in making your own. It's a luscious topping for waffles, pancakes, crepes, or ice cream, and keeps for up to two months in the refrigerator.

*2 teaspoons cornstarch*
*½ teaspoon baking soda*
*4 cups whole milk*
*4 cups goat's milk*
*2 cups sugar*
*1 3- to 4-inch Mexican cinnamon stick* ✽

Dissolve cornstarch and baking soda in 2 cups of the whole milk and set aside. In a heavy, 4-quart nonreactive saucepan, combine the remaining whole milk with the goat's milk and bring to a boil. Remove from heat and whisk in the reserved cornstarch-soda mixture (be careful; it is likely to foam up). Whisk in the sugar, add the cinnamon, and return to medium-high heat. Cook for about 1 hour, stirring often, or until the mixture has thickened enough to coat the back of a wooden spoon. Remove from heat and set aside at room temperature to cool completely; refrigerate in a covered jar. Makes 3 cups.

# NATILLA
## Vanilla Custard

On the Hacienda Sunday Brunch Buffet, this simple vanilla custard is always served next to a bowl of fresh fruit. It is also a worthy accompaniment to an assortment of cookies or a buttery pound cake.

*6 cups whole milk*
*1 Mexican vanilla bean, split lengthwise* ✽
*2 tablespoons Mexican vanilla extract* ✽
*8 egg yolks*
*1½ cups sugar*
*¼ cup cornstarch*

In a heavy, 4-quart nonreactive saucepan, combine the milk, vanilla bean, and vanilla extract. Bring to a boil, stirring often to prevent scorching; remove from heat and set aside. In a mixing bowl, beat the egg yolks and sugar until the mixture is thickened and pale in color. Add cornstarch gradually and beat until smooth. Whisking constantly, add about 2 cups of the hot milk mixture to the egg mixture to temper the eggs. Again whisking constantly, add the tempered egg mixture to the remaining hot milk. Return saucepan to heat. Cook over medium heat, stirring regularly, until the mixture thickens, about 15 to 20 minutes. Remove vanilla bean. Pour custard into a bowl and cover with plastic wrap, allowing it to touch the surface of the custard (so a skin will not form). Chill at least 1 hour. Serve chilled with fresh fruit, cookies, or pound cake. Makes about 1½ quarts.

# MANGOS FLAMEADOS ❀
## Flamed Mangoes over Ice Cream

Miguel adapted this classy flaming dessert from a recipe that Diana Kennedy discovered years ago at a hotel in Monterrey. It makes use of several delicious tropical flavors—mangoes, citrus juices, Mexican cinnamon, and tequila. For cooks with a dramatic flair, this dish can be prepared in a chafing dish and flamed at table side. At Fonda San Miguel, the mangoes are prepared to order in the kitchen and served over scoops of ice cream in a balloon wine glass. It makes a romantic dessert, and the generous portion is just enough to be shared by two.

*Half of an orange*

*Half of a lime*

*1 tablespoon butter*

*1 tablespoon granulated sugar*

*2 4-inch Mexican cinnamon sticks* ❀

*2 mango halves (fresh or canned), cut into chunks* ❀

*1 ounce orange liqueur, such as Cointreau or Triple Sec*

*1 ounce tequila*

*2 scoops vanilla or coconut ice cream*

Using a sharp paring knife or zester, remove the zest from the citrus fruits in thin strips and set aside. Squeeze the juice of the citrus fruits and combine to yield 3 to 4 tablespoons of juice. In a 10-inch, nonreactive sauté pan over medium heat, melt butter until it bubbles. Add the sugar and stir to dissolve. Add the citrus zest, juice, and cinnamon sticks. Heat the liquid over medium heat until it begins to thicken and turn a slightly golden color. Add the mangoes and heat through. Remove the cinnamon sticks. Add the liqueur and tequila and flame the liquid. Once the flame dies out, put ice cream in a balloon wine or parfait glass and top with hot fruit. Serve immediately. Serves 1 or 2.

José Fors

*Frutas*, 1995.
Oil on canvas,
39 × 26 inches.

*This surreal bowl of fruit
with a blue background
is one of the restaurant's
most exquisite paintings—
very sophisticated, very
subtle. José Fors usually
paints human figures, so
Frutas may be his only still
life. Like El chile, our other
Fors painting, this work
was purchased from Gal-
erie Ravel in Austin.*

T.G.

## CAJETA ICE CREAM

Tom discovered *cajeta* ice cream at a pastry shop in Oaxaca called Roma, and he insisted that it be re-created for the restaurant. It's delicious on its own or as the ice cream for Crepas de Cajeta.

*1¼ cups milk*

*1 Mexican vanilla bean, split lengthwise* ✻

*4 egg yolks*

*⅓ cup sugar*

*1¼ cups heavy cream*

*2 cups cajeta (see separate recipe) or prepared Coronado cajeta* ✻

*2 tablespoons sour cream*

*2 tablespoons Kahlua coffee liqueur*

*2 tablespoons butter*

*1 teaspoon Mexican vanilla extract* ✻

*3 tablespoons sliced almonds, toasted and crushed*

In a heavy, 1½-quart saucepan, combine milk and vanilla bean. Over medium heat, scald the milk, remove from heat, and set aside to steep for 5 minutes. In a medium mixing bowl, beat the egg yolks and sugar until very light in color. Remove vanilla bean from milk and, whisking constantly, pour some of the hot milk into the egg mixture; blend well. Pour the warmed egg and milk mixture back into the saucepan, whisking thoroughly. Cook over medium-low heat, stirring often, until mixture thickens enough to coat the back of a spoon, about 5 to 7 minutes. Remove from heat and cover with plastic wrap, allowing wrap to touch the surface of the custard (so a skin will not form). Set aside to cool at room temperature. When the custard has cooled completely, whisk in heavy cream and refrigerate. In a small, heavy saucepan, combine *cajeta*, sour cream, liqueur, butter, and vanilla extract and cook over medium heat until butter melts. Stir well and set aside to cool. Fold the cooled *cajeta* mixture into the custard and fold in the crushed almonds. Process according to the directions of your ice cream maker. Freeze until firm. Makes 1½ quarts.

## COCONUT ICE CREAM

This ice cream goes well with Mangoes Flameados. Cream of coconut is available in liquor stores as well as some Hispanic and Thai markets.

*4 large egg yolks*

*¾ cup sugar*

*1 cup half-and-half*

*1 teaspoon Mexican vanilla extract* ✻

*1 15-ounce can cream of coconut (about 2 cups)*

*2 cups heavy cream*

*¼ cup sweetened shredded coconut, toasted*

In the top of a double boiler, beat together egg yolks, sugar, half-and-half, and vanilla. Place the pan over simmering water and beat the mixture until it thickens and almost doubles in volume, about 10 minutes. Remove from heat, beat in the cream of coconut, cover, and refrigerate for at least 1 hour. When mixture is completely chilled, whisk in the heavy cream and coconut. Process according to the directions of your ice cream maker. Freeze until firm. Makes 1½ quarts.

# CHOCOLATE SORBET

When Fonda San Miguel opened, the established dessert tradition in Tex-Mex restaurants was a serving of lime, pineapple, or rainbow sherbet or a praline at the checkout counter. This elegant sorbet is a far cry from that. Miguel's partner, Philippe Mercier, has developed many other delectable sorbet recipes for the restaurant, and they are always in demand.

*4 cups water*
*1¾ cups sugar*
*1 pound Callebaut bittersweet chocolate, cut into small chunks*
*1 cup unsweetened cocoa*
*1 tablespoon Kahlua coffee liqueur*

In a heavy, 3-quart saucepan, bring water and sugar to a boil and cook over medium-high heat for 4 minutes to form a syrup. Remove from heat. Combine chopped chocolate, cocoa, and liqueur in a mixing bowl and whisk in the hot sugar syrup until mixture is smooth and the chocolate has melted. Do not overbeat or mixture will be grainy. Place bowl in a larger bowl filled with enough ice water to come halfway up the side of the smaller bowl. Stir often until completely cool. Process according to the directions of your ice cream maker. Freeze until firm. Makes 1½ quarts.

# MANGO SORBET

This sorbet makes a wonderful light ending to a meal.

*¾ cup water*
*1 cup sugar*
*3 ripe mangoes (about 1½ pounds), peeled and pitted* ✽
*Juice of 1 lime*

In a small, heavy saucepan bring the water and sugar to a boil. Set aside to cool. Put the mango pulp into a blender, add the cooled syrup and lime juice, and puree until smooth. Place bowl in a larger bowl filled with enough ice water to come halfway up the side of the smaller bowl. Stir often until completely cool. Process according to the directions of your ice cream maker. Freeze until firm. Makes 1 quart.

## Rodolfo Morales

*Untitled,* ca. 1990. Collage,
13½ × 19 inches.

*The collages of Rodolfo Morales are always great fun. To make his collages, Morales would ask peo-
ple to bring him all sorts of things—clippings from newspapers, string, bits of colored paper, tinfoil.
He utilized everything. He kept these various materials in big drawers, and when he was motivated,
he would put a collage together. These collages were his attempts to give common people, especially the poor, a way to buy his work. He sold the collages for the equivalent of about two hundred
to five hundred dollars. Now they sell for much more, of course. We've displayed these collages on
a wall with an oil portrait of Rodolfo Morales by Gordon Rayner. The works are positioned so that
he seems to be looking down at his own collages. Morales, who was from Oaxaca, was one of Mexico's most successful artists as well as a remarkable humanitarian. Before he achieved critical acclaim
painting primitive paintings using rich, vivid colors, he earned his living as a house painter. One of
his biggest fans was Stanley Marcus of Dallas, an avid collector of Mexican art.*

*T.G.*

# POLVORONES ESTILO SRA. ERÉNDIRA TERÁN LEVIN
## Mexican Wedding Cookies

*Polvorones* are the classic Mexican wedding cookies that are so popular everywhere they are made. Fonda San Miguel is proud to present this family recipe given to us by our dear friend, Señora Eréndira Terán Levin.

*1 stick butter, softened at room temperature*

*½ cup powdered sugar*

*1 cup all-purpose white flour*

*1 cup pecans, finely chopped in blender or food processor*

*Extra powdered sugar for coating the* polvorones *after baking*

Position one oven rack in the top third of your oven and the second rack in the bottom third. Preheat oven to 350 degrees.

Prepare two baking sheets by lining with parchment paper.

In a large bowl, lightly cream the butter with a spatula or the back of a spoon.

Incorporate all of the dry ingredients except the pecans into the butter, mixing well with your hands. Then add the pecans and continue to mix with your hands until they are completely folded into the dough. Chill the dough in the refrigerator for approximately 30 minutes.

While the dough is chilling, sift the extra powdered sugar into a medium bowl.

Break off pieces of dough that measure approximately 1 level tablespoon. Using your fingers, form small logs of dough, approximately 3 inches long. Put a little pressure on the end of each log so that it is pointed.

Arrange the logs (forming them into "smiles") about 1 inch apart on the baking sheets. Bake for 15 minutes, or until light golden brown. Watch to make sure they do not overcook. Allow the cookies to cool on the baking sheets for 5 minutes.

When the cookies are lightly browned, remove them from the baking sheets and, while they are still warm, roll them in the extra powdered sugar until they are thickly coated and silky. You might like to roll them in the powdered sugar a second time after they cool.

The cookies will keep in a tightly covered tin for about one week. Makes approximately 3 dozen cookies.

# BURGUNDY-POACHED PEARS

These ruby-colored pears are every bit as lovely as they are delicious when served for dessert after a hearty brunch or elegant dinner. Serve them with a dollop of whipped cream.

> *1 quart burgundy wine*
> *1 quart water*
> *1 8-ounce cone piloncillo, grated* ✽
> *1 3-inch Mexican cinnamon stick* ✽
> *1 tablespoon Mexican vanilla extract* ✽
> *8 firm Bartlett pears, peeled, with stems left on*

In a deep, 4-quart nonreactive saucepan, combine all ingredients except the pears and bring to a boil. Reduce heat to low and cook for about 1 hour. Add pears and poach an additional 15 to 20 minutes. (Weight the pears down with a plate so they will remain submerged in the syrup and absorb the color evenly.) Do not overcook. Remove from heat and allow pears to cool in the syrup for about 1 hour. Carefully remove with a slotted spoon and refrigerate until ready to serve. Serve chilled. Serves 8.

# ROMPOPE
## Mexican Eggnog

Rompope, the ultra-rich Mexican eggnog, is another creation credited to the legendary nuns of Puebla. Bottled commercial versions of the liqueur are available all over Mexico, and it is a very popular holiday libation. Many families make their own rendition, and Miguel's family is no exception. His grandmother served it in small brandy glasses after meals during the Christmas holidays.

> *8 cups plus ½ cup whole milk*
> *2 cups sugar*
> *8 egg yolks*
> *2 3-inch Mexican cinnamon sticks* ✽
> *Presidente brandy to taste (optional)*
> *Pinch of ground cinnamon or nutmeg*

In a heavy, 4-quart, nonreactive saucepan, combine the 8 cups milk and sugar over medium-high heat. Bring to a boil, reduce heat to low, and cook for about 15 minutes, stirring often to prevent scorching. In a medium bowl, whisk together egg yolks and the remaining ½ cup milk. Whisking constantly, add about 1 cup of the hot milk mixture to the egg yolks. Then whisk the warmed egg mixture into the hot milk mixture. Add the cinnamon sticks and cook over low heat until the mixture thickens enough to coat the back of a spoon, about 4 to 5 minutes. Remove from heat, whisk in the brandy, and cool completely before serving. Serve chilled in small brandy glasses with a pinch of cinnamon. Serves 12. Makes 2½ quarts.

# CAFÉ DE OLLA
## Coffee in the Pot

A popular hot drink with its own ritual, Café de Olla is a traditional after-dinner drink. The dark, sweet brew is made with coffee, spices, and sugar boiled together in a pot. The sugar is in the form of cones of *piloncillo*, Mexican brown sugar. When this beverage is served in the morning or to children, it is often diluted with steamed milk.

> *6 cups water*
>
> *1 3-inch Mexican cinnamon stick* ❀
>
> *2 whole cloves*
>
> *3 ounces* piloncillo, *grated, or ¾ cup dark brown sugar* ❀
>
> *3 ounces dark-roast, regular-grind coffee (about 6 tablespoons)*

In a heavy, 3-quart, nonreactive saucepan, heat the water, cinnamon, cloves, and sugar over medium-high heat, stirring until sugar is dissolved. Add coffee and bring to a boil, reduce heat, and simmer 3 minutes. Remove from heat, cover, and allow to steep 3 to 5 minutes. Strain through a fine sieve or coffee filter into warm mugs. Serves 6.

# CHOCOLATE A LA MEXICANA
## Mexican Hot Chocolate

Hot chocolate is a centuries-old tradition in Mexico with its own ritual and special equipment. Many families have a special chocolate pot and a decoratively carved wooden *molinillo* to insert into the pot and rotate between the palms to create foam. (A whisk between the palms or an immersion blender works well, too.) The chocolate bars traditionally used to make this drink contain ground sugar, cinnamon, and, in some cases, ground nuts. Miguel's favorite brand is Abuelita, but several other brands are usually available.

> *4 cups whole milk*
>
> *1 3-ounce square Mexican chocolate* ❀

In a heavy, 3-quart, nonreactive saucepan, heat the milk over low heat. Add chocolate and cook until melted, stirring regularly so the mixture won't stick to the bottom of the pan. Once the chocolate is melted, bring the mixture to a boil. Remove from heat, pour into a chocolate pot or ceramic pitcher, and use a *molinillo* to foam the liquid, rotating it back and forth between the palms of your hands. You can also leave the mixture in the saucepan and use a whisk or immersion blender to beat the liquid until foamy. Serve in warm mugs. Serves 4.

# Acknowledgments

We are grateful to everyone whose enthusiastic support and specialized talents contributed to the success of Fonda San Miguel:

Chris Adams
Oscar Álvarez
Paul & Natalie Bardagjy
J. B. and Marilyn Bell
Paula Biehler
Chris Bratcher
Rose Cardona
Lisa C. Ellis
Royce Flournoy
Cindy Goldman
Jay Hargrave
Janice Harris
Victoria Hentrich
Danny Herrera

Lucinda Hutson
Diana Kennedy
Endy Teran Levin
Bill Luft
Philippe Mercier
Beatrice Moore
Elizabeth Morris
Pamela Nevarez
Margaret Parker
Gloria Pennington
Ana Pool
Forrest Preece
Patricia Quintana
Mercedes Ramos

Dana Ravel
Wilfrido Rodríguez
Amalia Rodriguez-Mendoza
John Roegnik
Roberto Santibáñez
Frank Seely
María Dolores Torres Yzabal
Susana Trilling
Matt Wiessler
Peter Withers
and
The many esteemed guests of
Fonda San Miguel over the
years

We especially want to thank Virginia Wood for writing the first edition of this book. She knows the history of Fonda San Miguel as well as anyone, and her ideas, tenacious energy, and excellent writing made this book possible. We are forever in her debt.

For this new edition, Cristina Potters stepped in and continued with the same skill and dedication, for which we are eternally grateful.

We have benefited from the skill and hard work of so many people in the restaurant's history that it is impossible to acknowledge them all. We regret the omissions.

M.R.
T.G.

# The People of Fonda San Miguel

## STEVEN ADAMS

Steven Adams is an example of a very rare thing in the American restaurant industry—a mature man who considers wait service his profession and approaches the work with the professionalism it deserves. "I have a family and many other interests, but waiting tables is how I earn my living," Steven explains. He came to Fonda San Miguel from Santa Fe's Coyote Café in early 1992, the result of a decision to return his then-young family to Austin for better educational opportunities. Steven is now one of a core group of longtime servers who take a leadership role in mentoring new staff members and setting an example for the Fonda San Miguel style of customer service. That could explain why he's one of Fonda San Miguel's most popular waiters—with a long list of regular customers requesting his service every time they visit the restaurant. "This restaurant has a very loyal clientele. I'm certainly not the only waiter who has regulars; many of us do," Steven says modestly, adding, "If you look out for them and take care of their particular needs, they take care of you." Steven describes himself as a "foodie" and proudly says he does the grocery shopping and cooking for his family. Grilling and making soups are his favorite culinary adventures. He admits he was an avowed fan of Fonda San Miguel's cuisine long before he became an employee. "I like stability in my life, and staying with one job helps provide that," Steven says of his long tenure at Fonda San Miguel. "I feel my most important contribution to the restaurant is my ability to focus on client contact." Indeed, Fonda San Miguel prides itself on a lower-than-average staff turnover and consistent customer service. Steven Adams and waiters like him have a lot to do with that.

## OSCAR ÁLVAREZ

Oscar Álvarez arrived in Austin at the age of nineteen. He had left his home in Zacatecas, Mexico, with the strong desire to find work in the United States and the name of a cousin who already had a job here. As luck would have it, Oscar's cousin, Zenón Rentería, worked in a Mexican restaurant with an opening in the kitchen. Oscar started out in the lowest prep job in the Fonda San Miguel kitchen twenty years ago. During

his tenure at the restaurant, he's worked at every station in the kitchen and is now executive sous chef. Oscar's day begins at 1:00 p.m. when he comes in to check how the morning prep crew's work is coming along and gets started on his own long list with his crew on the second shift. Late in the afternoon, he oversees the line setup, and when service begins, he runs the line, making sure orders are assembled quickly and correctly. At the end of the evening, he does an inventory, makes the next day's orders, and heads home. "I learned a little cooking from my mother before I left home," Oscar recalls, "but it was really Miguel who taught me everything I know." As Miguel's trusted right hand, Oscar has represented the restaurant at two James Beard House events—in 1993 and 1995—where he helped to prepare meals that wowed the New York crowd. "New York is quite a city. It was exciting! We went to the top of the Towers; we ate at Patria. I learned a lot working in the Beard House kitchen." Oscar Álvarez is one of a small fraternity of Austin chefs who can make that claim. He also assisted chef Roberto Santibáñez in the preparation of meals at a Mexican food festival presented by the Mexican Embassy in Australia in 2000.

Fonda San Miguel has provided Oscar with not only a career but also a family. His wife, Gerarda Salazar, worked in the kitchen, making salads. "That's how we met," Oscar says with a smile. These days Gerarda is at home with their daughter Stephanie and their sons, José Manuel and Oscar Jr. Gerarda's daughter Lila works part time in the Fonda San Miguel office and spends some evenings at the hostess stand as well, making her a second-generation Fonda San Miguel employee. Like many of the Mexican nationals employed in the kitchen, Oscar got his official papers during the immigration amnesty of the mid-1980s, so it's easy for him to take his family home to Zacatecas for yearly visits in August when business at the restaurant is slower. He doesn't do much cooking at home, but when he is cooking for himself from the Fonda San Miguel menu, he's partial to Camarones al Mojo de Ajo.

# GORKY GONZÁLEZ

Gorky González is famous throughout Mexico for his unique Majolica pottery and ceramic tiles. As a young man he studied sculpture with his father, the renowned sculptor Rodolfo González, and also traveled to Japan to study ceramic techniques. Gorky is known in Mexico as the artisan who preserved the traditional Majolica pottery techniques for which the area around Guanajuato was once famous. He located his studio there and returned to the use of traditional formulas and techniques to revive the lost art of the popular pottery. He uses clay extracted from the nearby Santa Rosa Mountains. His pieces are formed in molds, by hand, or on a potter's wheel and fired first in a brick kiln to prepare for the enameling process. Gorky uses only locally prepared, mineral-based special ceramic enamel paints on his pieces. Each piece is painted by hand with cat-hair brushes imported from the Far East, using no stencils or patterns. The second firing forges the enamel to the pottery forming a distinctive glaze. By 1978 Tom had begun collecting the Mexican folk art pieces that became a crucial element of the restaurant's design. In 1979 Diana Kennedy took Miguel and Tom on a pilgrimage to Guanajuato to select folk art for the restaurant, and Gorky's studio was at the top of their itinerary. "His workshop studio was in the courtyard of his home," Tom recalls. "On that first visit, we bought a number of plates with 'Fonda San Miguel' painted on them, and we still have many of those," Tom remembers. "We weren't as lucky with some of the first pots and jars, but over the years, we've collected more of Gorky's work." Many of the ceramic platters and dishes on the Sunday buffet are Gorky González designs. The recent tile work around the front door, the tortilla station, the patio, and the large dining room are original González designs commissioned especially for the restaurant. "We've done business with Gorky for so long that now we've gotten to know his son, young Gorky, who helps him in the business. It's great to have that continuity," says Tom with pride.

# JANICE HARRIS

Janice Harris was in high school when her older brother David became friends with Tom Gilliland and Miguel Ravago, then proprietors of the San Angel Inn in Houston. She became their friend, too, and maintained the relationship after they left Houston for Austin. She became a frequent visitor to the restaurant over the years, especially while living in San Antonio. She moved to Austin in the early 1980s to work for an insurance company, but spent many evenings and weekends at the Fonda San Miguel front desk, running credit card charges for the waiters, long before such things were done immediately by computer. She eventually moved back to San Antonio but dropped into the restaurant to visit from time to time. She was passing through Austin in the summer of 1995 when Tom surprised her with an offer. "He told me over dinner one night that the office manager was leaving and asked whether I would be interested in taking over that position," Janice recalls. "At first, I didn't take it very seriously, but by the time I got back home to San Antonio, I'd managed to talk myself into it." Janice has been the office manager at Fonda San Miguel since August of 1995. The very nature of the restaurant business is one of tempest and upheaval, but Janice can always be counted on to be the calm center of the storm. Whatever you need to know about the day-to-day business of Fonda San Miguel, she's the go-to gal.

Opposite: The "Heart of the House."

## LUCINDA HUTSON

Lucinda Hutson is a native of El Paso who speaks fluent Spanish and has traveled extensively in Mexico throughout her life. An accomplished gardener and herbalist with an anthropology degree from the University of Texas at Austin, Hutson authored *The Herb Garden Cookbook*. It is the foremost resource on growing and cooking with herbs of the Southwest. Another aspect of Lucinda's career has been teaching. She first taught classes about cooking with Southwestern herbs at Ann Clark's La Bonne Cuisine Cooking School at Bon Appetite Cookware in Austin in the 1980s. Miguel Ravago was a student in one of her classes, and they became fast friends. "I'd never been a fan of Tex-Mex food, so at first I was pretty skeptical when I heard about two guys who had opened a restaurant supposedly serving the food of Mexico's interior," Lucinda recalls. Once she and Miguel became friends, however, Lucinda became a Fonda San Miguel regular, eventually designing and installing the restaurant's first herb garden. Lucinda's second book would be an inviting and informative work about tequila. *Tequila! Cooking with the Spirit of Mexico* was filled with tequila history, lore, and folktales as well as a unique collection of recipes. Illustrated with Lucinda's own extensive collection of Mexican folk art, the book was expanded and updated in 2013 as *¡Viva Tequila!* As a tequila expert, Lucinda consulted with Tom and Miguel on selecting the finest tequilas for the restaurant's bar. The debut of the tequila book coincided with an invitation for Fonda San Miguel to present the Hacienda Buffet at the prestigious James Beard House in New York in 1995. Tom and Miguel invited Lucinda to add her expert tequila presentation to the event, and her glorious, festive punches were a huge hit. These days she tends her much-photographed garden and contributes articles to prominent cooking and gardening magazines. She is a popular speaker at venues as diverse as the Smithsonian Institute, the National Herb Society, the Central Market Cooking Schools, and the Lake Austin Spa Resort.

## BILL LUFT

In the early 1970s, many discerning Austinites with a taste for elegant Mexican art objects, housewares, and furnishings shopped at stores in Laredo and Puerto Vallarta called La Casona. Interior designer Bill Luft was the owner and creative genius at La Casona. Mutual friends took Tom Gilliland shopping in the Laredo store and a long friendship blossomed. "Bill's particular gift is for merchandising—the way he arranged and presented things in those stores made it possible for you to imagine how something was going to look when you got it home," Tom explains. By 1978, the owners of Fonda San Miguel began to experience their first success. Tom and Miguel were eager to remodel the restaurant and begin to create the decor and folk art collection for which it would become famous. "The first time we could afford for someone to help us decorate, we were lucky that Bill was so knowledgeable about Mexican design and that he knew all the best sources," says Tom. That first venture in 1978 was the beginning of a long creative collaboration. "Bill lets me collect the art work because he thinks I'm better at that," Tom explains, "and then he comes up periodically and arranges things." In fact, Tom credits Bill Luft's vision and talents as an interior designer for the visual ambience that defines Fonda San Miguel. Bill maintains a busy schedule as a designer in Mexico and the United States.

# JESÚS "CHUCHO" MORENO

When Chucho Moreno dropped into Fonda San Miguel for brunch in the spring of 2004, he had no way of knowing just how pleased Tom and Miguel would be to see him. The talented Mexican colorist had painted the restaurant's interior in the mid-eighties under Bill Luft's tutelage. With the interior renovation of the restaurant in full swing, Tom had been thinking about how much he'd like to have Chucho spruce up the restaurant, but he had no idea how to contact him. When the two had a chance to talk, the first thing Chucho said was, "It's been about twenty years since the early design; I think it's time for me to come back!" That was exactly what Tom had in mind. A deal was struck, and Chucho was soon moving his scaffolding from room to room, working his magic on the interior walls.

Forty-six-year-old Chucho Moreno is a native of Mexico City who studied art and graphic design at the University of Mexico (UNAM) and sculpture and art restoration at the Escuela Nacional de Artes Plásticas. Chucho's talents have brought commissions from all over Mexico, Europe, and the United States. His skills as an art restorer put him in great demand for work on monuments and paintings at the Museo Nacional de Antropología e Historia (INAH) as well as the colonial history museum in El Castillo de Chapultepec, the famed castle in Mexico City's Chapultepec Park. The top film and theater directors in Mexico solicit his painting expertise on sets for movies and theatrical productions.

Chucho's many years in art restoration helped him develop the skills that define the style of work he's done at Fonda San Miguel. He uses washes of color on the stucco walls to achieve the appearance of weathered surfaces and then enhances the walls with incredibly detailed freehand stenciling. Chucho spent several months at Fonda San Miguel in 2004 creating a distinctive new look for the interior of the restaurant as it moved into its fourth decade. For example, the patio bar has sun-washed yellow walls detailed with faded blue urns of flowers, while some of the walls in the main dining room are decorated with a border of angels, each uniquely specific to Austin and Fonda San Miguel. Once the Fonda project was completed, Chucho was off to Mexico to reunite with his family.

# MERCEDES RAMOS

The most striking thing about Mercedes Ramos is that she looks as though she could have stepped right out of one of the Zúñiga paintings hanging in the dining room. Aesthetically and personally, the diminutive grandmother is perfectly at home inside Fonda San Miguel's front door. After more than twenty-five years at the host stand, for many people the face of Mercedes is the most identifiable one at the restaurant. There are plenty of customers who will swear that Mercy is Miguel's mother and others who are equally convinced that Tom is her son. There are no family ties at all, of course, although Tom and Mercy have been friends since he was a law student in Austin in the 1960s. That's how the long relationship began. Mercy and her five sisters worked at the old Tower Drug Store, once located just north of the University of Texas law school. Tom ate lunch there several times a week. He was well acquainted with the Ramos sisters, and their friendly style of customer service made a lasting impression on him. Tom ran into Mercedes years later when he returned to Austin to open Fonda San Miguel. Although he initially wasn't sure which Ramos sister she was, he offered her a job on the spot. After a dinner visit to the restaurant with her family, Mercedes said yes. She's been at the host stand pretty much ever since, calling people "honey" in that sweet grandmotherly way that soothes the sometimes lengthy wait for a table. She did try retirement in the late 1990s, but customer demand brought her back a few nights a week.

## PACO

Fonda San Miguel's raucous parrot, Paco, is a popular attraction, especially among children. He has been a resident of the restaurant's patio since the early 1990s, when he was acquired to replace a predecessor named Fagin. Although Paco has never received any formal speech training, he knows how to entertain with his vocal antics and brash showmanship. Long-time employee Willie Rodríguez is Paco's primary caregiver. Double Yellowhead Amazon parrots like Paco are native to central Mexico.

## Teódulo Rómulo

*Untitled, 1980. Mixograph, 19 × 47 inches.*

*An artist whose name I love to pronounce is Teódulo Rómulo, the creator of this unusual print. The style is very contemporary, with an odd little square figure in the center and the fanciful cow/pig creature to the right. The stunning print is also beautifully framed. I jokingly call it "The Purple People Eater." The print was originally purchased from Galerie Ravel by a local physician. When he began to pare down his art collection, he came to me and asked whether I would like to buy the print. It was a work I had admired for many years, so I jumped at the chance. Rómulo, a painter and printmaker from Mexico City, actually spent six months painting in Austin when gallery owner Dana Ravel and her husband Gene brought him here for a sabbatical.*

*T.G.*

# Basic Preparations

Every cuisine has its basic components, building blocks that contribute to the successful presentation of a complete meal. The depth of flavor in many of the restaurant's recipes depends on the foundation of a rich, homemade chicken stock. Several dishes are enhanced by the companionship of a fresh, tasty salsa, and servings of hearty rice and bean dishes round out most meals. At Fonda San Miguel everything is made from scratch, and it takes Miguel, sous chef Oscar Álvarez, and a staff of eight to prepare the menu every day. However, once the home cook masters a few basic dishes to accompany a show-stopping main course, it will be possible to turn out an entire Fonda San Miguel–style meal without a full prep staff as backup.

## BASIC CHICKEN BROTH

This is Miguel's all-purpose chicken stock recipe. It is a rich, flavorful foundation on which many other recipes are built. Although it is time-consuming to make, it will add depth of flavor to any recipe that calls for chicken broth or stock. The smart thing to do is make it in very large batches and freeze it in quart portions for future use.

*1 whole frying chicken, cut up*

*1 medium white onion, sliced*

*1 carrot, sliced*

*3 garlic cloves, mashed*

*8 whole black peppercorns*

*1 teaspoon sea salt*

Combine all ingredients in an 8-quart stock pot, add cold water to cover, and bring to a simmer over medium heat. Cook 35 to 45 minutes, or until chicken is tender. With a slotted spoon, remove chicken pieces and allow to cool. When cool enough to handle, remove the meat from the bones and refrigerate meat for another use. Return the bones to the broth and cook an additional 1 hour. Remove from heat and allow to cool to room temperature. Refrigerate the stock until fat solidifies on the surface, about 6 to 8 hours. Using a slotted spoon or skimmer, skim off fat from the surface of the stock. Strain before using. Makes 2 quarts.

## SALSA MEXICANA

This fresh, chunky salsa can be served as a dip for tortilla chips, a topping for quesadillas and taco fillings, or an accompaniment for grilled meats. It's a quick and easy little workhorse any way you look at it.

*4 serrano chiles, minced* ✿

*Half of a medium white onion, chopped*

*4 sprigs cilantro, stemmed and chopped*

*4 medium tomatoes, seeded and chopped*

*1 teaspoon sea salt*

*½ cup cold water*

Combine all ingredients in a medium nonreactive bowl; stir to mix well. Refrigerate until ready to serve. Serve chilled. Makes 4 cups.

## ARROZ BLANCO
### Basic White Rice

Although most people think all Mexican dishes are served with Arroz Mexicano—red or Spanish rice—many coastal seafood dishes are served with white rice. Miguel likes to garnish white rice with green peas for a splash of color.

*2 tablespoons safflower oil*

*2 cups long-grain white rice*

*4 cups Basic Chicken Broth (see separate recipe)*

*1 teaspoon sea salt or to taste*

*1 cup frozen green peas, thawed*

Heat oil in a heavy, 3-quart saucepan or Dutch oven over medium-high heat. Add rice. Stirring often with a wooden spoon, cook 8 to 10 minutes, or until rice is golden. Add chicken broth, reduce heat to medium, cover, and cook an additional 20 minutes, or until all liquid has been absorbed. Fluff with a fork and add salt, if necessary. Sprinkle with green peas and serve hot. Serves 8.

# ARROZ MEXICANO ❀
## Mexican Rice

This is Diana Kennedy's version of the well-known Mexican side dish. The process is time-consuming but yields delicious rice.

> 1½ cups long-grain white rice
>
> ⅓ cup vegetable oil
>
> 1 12-ounce can whole tomatoes in their juice
>
> Half of a medium white onion, chopped
>
> 2 cloves garlic, chopped
>
> 4 cups Basic Chicken Broth (see separate recipe)
>
> 1 teaspoon sea salt
>
> ½ cup frozen corn kernels
>
> ½ cup frozen green peas

Put rice in a large bowl, add hot water to cover, and allow to stand for about 25 minutes. Drain rice in a colander and rinse under cold running water. Shake well to remove excess water and set aside to allow the rice to dry. In a deep, heavy pot or Dutch oven, heat the oil over medium heat. Stirring occasionally, fry dried rice 8 to 10 minutes, or until the rice is a pale golden color. Drain off any excess oil and set pan aside. Combine tomatoes, onion, and garlic in a blender and puree until smooth. Return pan to heat and add the tomato puree; cook over high heat, stirring often, until almost dry, about 8 to 10 minutes. Stir in the broth, salt, corn, and peas. Reduce heat to medium and cook uncovered, without stirring, until most of the liquid has been absorbed, 20 to 30 minutes. (At this stage holes will appear in the surface.) Remove from heat, cover with foil, and set aside to soften, about 10 minutes. Serve hot. Serves 8.

# ARROZ VERDE
## Green Rice

The green color in this rice dish comes from poblano chiles, spinach, and fresh herbs. Mexican home cooks are likely to prepare it for holidays and other special occasions. The result will be moister than the other rice dishes in this book.

> 2 tablespoons safflower oil
>
> 2 cups long-grain white rice
>
> Half of a medium white onion, finely chopped
>
> 4 garlic cloves, minced
>
> ½ cup chopped cilantro leaves
>
> ½ cup chopped parsley leaves
>
> 4 spinach leaves, stemmed and chopped
>
> 1 poblano chile, roasted, peeled, seeded, and chopped ❀
>
> 2½ cups Basic Chicken Broth (see separate recipe)
>
> Sea salt and ground black pepper to taste

In a heavy, 4-quart saucepan or Dutch oven, heat oil over medium-high heat. Add rice, onion, and garlic. Stirring often with a wooden spoon, cook for about 8 to 10 minutes, or until rice is golden. In a blender, combine cilantro, parsley, spinach, chile, and chicken broth; blend until smooth. Add pureed mixture to sautéed rice, reduce heat to medium, cover, and cook for about 20 minutes, or until all liquid is absorbed. Fluff with a fork and adjust seasonings, adding salt and pepper if necessary. Serve hot. Serves 8.

# FRIJOLES NEGROS
## Black Beans

Black turtle beans are very common in the interior of Mexico and in the Caribbean. Fonda San Miguel introduced them to Austin diners. In the early days, beans arrived in 55-gallon containers directly from Mexico, as did many of the dried chiles. Today black beans and dried chiles are commonly found in grocery stores all over Austin. These beans are a hearty side dish and were the basis for the restaurant's first black bean nachos, made with Monterey Jack cheese and Salsa Mexicana. Frijoles Negros—sometimes known as Frijoles de Olla, or "beans in a pot"—refers to any variety of soupy beans.

*1 pound black turtle beans*

*10 cups water*

*Half of a medium white onion, sliced*

*3 tablespoons vegetable shortening or lard*

*2 sprigs fresh or dried epazote* ✿

*1 tablespoon sea salt or to taste*

Rinse the beans in a colander and pick through them to remove any small stones or clumps of dirt. Combine beans, water, onion, shortening, and epazote in a heavy, 8-quart stock pot and bring to a boil over medium-high heat. Reduce heat to low, cover, and simmer for 1½ hours, or until beans are tender but not mushy. Add salt. Makes 1½ quarts.

# FRIJOLES REFRITOS
## Refried Black Beans

Refried black beans make a rich and creamy companion for many entrées, especially when they are enhanced with a dollop of sour cream and a sprinkling of crumbled panela cheese. They are also a tasty topping for nachos and *sopes*.

*Frijoles Negros (see separate recipe)*

*6 tablespoons vegetable oil or lard*

*Half of a medium white onion, chopped*

*Sour cream for garnish*

*Crumbled panela cheese for garnish*

Drain the cooked beans, reserving ¾ to 1 cup of the cooking liquid. Mash beans with a potato masher. In a large, heavy skillet, heat the oil over medium heat, add onion, and cook until onion is wilted and transparent, about 5 to 6 minutes. Add mashed beans and up to 1 cup of the reserved cooking liquid; fry for about 5 minutes over medium heat, or until beans have absorbed the oil and there are no traces of unblended fat. Garnish with sour cream and crumbled panela cheese. Makes 4 to 5 cups.

# Unique Ingredients and Techniques

As the Hispanic population of America grows and migrates across the country, the ingredients necessary for preparing authentic Mexican dishes are becoming easier to locate. Many of the basic items that are unique to Mexican cuisine can be purchased in markets that serve a Hispanic clientele as well as from produce vendors and tortilla factories that service Mexican restaurants. Whereas most staples had to be imported directly from Mexico in the early years, Fonda San Miguel is now able to purchase nearly everything locally. If these products are not readily available in your area, consult the list of mail order sources in the next section.

Many of the fresh ingredients listed below, such as banana leaves, chile peppers, cactus pads, tomatillos, and pumpkin seeds, require special preparation techniques. Once mastered, these simple techniques will contribute authentic Mexican flavor and flair to your completed dishes. As a shopping guide, the preferred brand names of prepared foods are included in the list.

## Achiote

These bright red seeds from the annatto plant are an integral part of the cuisine of the Yucatan. They are most often ground into a paste and used in seasoning rubs. Both the seeds and the paste are available in Mexican markets. (El Yucateco brand)

## Banana Leaves

Banana leaves are used as wrappers for everything from tamales to barbecued meats, depending on which state of Mexico you visit. In the United States, banana leaves are found in the produce department of Hispanic grocery stores. Cut the leaves to the size required for your dish; use metal tongs to hold them over an open flame until they are pliable enough to be folded easily without breaking.

## Cajeta

This rich goat's-milk caramel is good over crepes, ice cream, waffles, or pancakes. Although a recipe for making your own is included in this book, good commercial brands are available. (Coronado brand)

## Cheese

Panela is a salty, feta-like cheese made from cow's milk and then dried and formed in shallow baskets. It is crumbled or cubed and sprinkled over some appetizers, enchiladas, and salads. Feta is an acceptable substitute.

## Chiles—Canned

Many of the recipes in this book call for chipotle chiles in adobo sauce. A chipotle chile is a red-ripe jalapeño that has been dried and smoked. The canned product features chipotles packed in a thick adobo sauce made from ancho chiles, tomatoes, and spices. (San Marcos brand)

Pickled jalapeños (*jalapeños en escabeche*) are whole jalapeños packed in tangy pickling brine, usually containing slices of carrot and pieces of onion as well. (San Marcos brand)

## Chiles—Dried

Three varieties of dried chiles are used in many recipes in this book. The ancho is a rust-colored dry chile, broad at the stem end and narrowing to a triangular tip; anchos are poblanos that have ripened to a dark red color and dried. Anchos are used in many sauces and two relleno dishes in this book. The mulato, a relative of the poblano, is dark brown and triangular. Ripened to a chocolate brown and dried, it is used in mole sauces. The shiny black pasilla chile, a dried chilaca chile, is narrow and five to six inches long. Pasillas are used in sauces as well as fried and crumbled for a garnish.

Good-quality dried chiles should still be fragrant and pliable. Wipe them carefully with a damp cloth or paper towel to remove any dust. It's a good idea to wear rubber gloves when handling all chiles.

To seed dried chiles, use a sharp paring knife to make a slit down the side and carefully scrape out the seeds.

To fry dried chiles for sauces, heat oil to shimmering and fry chiles for 10 to 15 seconds, turning once. (Don't allow them to burn, or the resulting sauce will be bitter.) Remove and drain on paper towels.

To toast dried chiles, place them on a hot comal or dry skillet for 10 to 15 seconds; turn them once or twice, being careful not to burn them. After frying or toasting, chiles can be rehydrated by soaking them in very hot water for 15 to 20 minutes.

## Chiles—Fresh

Jalapeños are probably the most recognizable Mexican chile and the easiest to find in the United States. The jalapeño is a fat, bullet-shaped, deep green chile, two to three inches long. In sauces, jalapeños can be substituted for serranos. The poblano is dark green, five to six inches long, and triangular in shape, with a wide stem end. Strips of roasted poblanos are made into *rajas* and are the basis for many chile relleno dishes. Serranos are thin, bullet-shaped chiles, dark green in color and two to three inches in length. Raw or roasted serranos add heat and flavor to many sauces.

Fresh chiles can be roasted until charred and blistered on a dry comal, under a broiler, or over an open flame, using tongs. For *rajas* and rellenos, put charred poblano chiles in a plastic bag and allow them to sweat for 10 to 15 minutes. Using rubber gloves, peel off the charred outer skin. (Do not peel chiles under running water or much of the roasted flavor will be lost.) For rellenos, cut a slit down one side from the shoulder to the tip and scrape out the seeds and membranes, being careful to keep the chile as intact as possible. For *rajas*, cut off the stem end and slice the peppers lengthwise into thin, ¼-inch strips. (Don't rub your eyes, nose, mouth, or other tender body areas while handling chiles. Capsaicin, the volatile substance that gives chiles their pungency, is stored in the seeds and membranes and will burn the skin.)

## Chocolate

Mexican chocolate has a consistency that is completely different from the product to which we are accustomed in this country. It is pressed into squares with sugar and sometimes ground nuts and spices. Chop or grate it before adding it to sauces or milk for hot chocolate. (Abuelita brand)

## Chorizo

Mexican chorizo is a soft, crumbly pork sausage flavored with chiles and spices. The best homemade chorizo uses lean, tender pork whereas the commercial varieties are often made with cheap cuts and pork trimmings. Some brands contain more fat and gristle than others, so it may take some research to find one that is appealing. Remove the required amount of sausage from the casing and place in a skillet over medium-low heat. Fry for 6 to 8 minutes to brown the meat and render the fat. Drain the fat and proceed with the recipe.

## Cinnamon (Canela)

Although it is not native to Mexico, what we refer to as "Mexican cinnamon," often labeled "canela," is the bark of the true cinnamon plant native to Ceylon (now Sri Lanka). Sold in very thin, somewhat flaky, curled sticks, it is the preferred variety for all the recipes in this book calling for cinnamon.

## Corn Husks

Corn husks are used to wrap many varieties of tamales. Cover dry corn husks with boiling water and allow them to soak for 15 to 20 minutes, or until they are pliable. Drain and pat dry. Spread with masa and fill with a tamale filling.

## Epazote

In Mexican folk wisdom this pungent herb is prescribed for gastric distress and flatulence, which is probably why it is added to beans while they are cooking. It is never eaten raw. It grows wild in Mexico and the southwestern United States and is easy to grow in herb gardens.

## Huitlacoche

This purple-blue fungus, also spelled "cuitlacoche," grows on corn and is a great culinary delicacy in Mexico. We've only found one source for fresh huitlacoche in the United States, Burns Farm in Florida, but good canned and frozen products are available in Hispanic markets and via mail order. Prepare according to the directions on the package. (La Costeña brand)

## Mangoes

This sweet, juicy tropical fruit is most likely to be available fresh in the United States during the summer months. To easily peel fresh mangoes, cut from end to end on either side of the flat pit in the center of the fruit, releasing the fruit from the pit. Score the fruit in chunks or strips and release from the peel using a spoon. Canned mangoes packed in syrup are available year round and should be drained completely before using in any recipes in this book.

## Nopales

When purchasing fresh prickly pear cactus pads in Hispanic markets, make sure they are bright green, firm, and between ¼ and ½ inch thick. Handle very carefully to avoid the thin, hair-like thorns! Use a sharp knife or vegetable peeler to trim the outside edges of the pads and scrape the thorns off both sides. Wash thoroughly and cut into strips or small pieces. Most recipes call for cooked *nopales*. Many cooks boil them in salted water for 15 to 20 minutes and then rinse under cold water to wash away their slimy, okra-like liquid. In her book *From My Mexican Kitchen,* Diana Kennedy claims that steaming the *nopales* for 8 to 10 minutes is preferable because it allows the to retain their flavor, texture, and nutritional value. For grilled *nopales,* score the pads lengthwise on both sides, oil very lightly, and place on a hot grill or comal. Cook 3 to 4 minutes on each side, depending on thickness. Fresh *nopalitos* in plastic bags are available in the produce department of some Hispanic markets. Slices of *nopales* are also sold in jars. (San Marcos brand)

## Piloncillo

This dark, unrefined Mexican sugar is sold in solid cones of various sizes (recipes in this book call for 8-ounce cones). For best results, grate the sugar before adding it to recipes.

## Pumpkin Seeds (Pepitas)

The recipes in this book call for hulled pumpkin seeds. When frying or toasting pumpkin seeds in a dry skillet or on a comal, keep a cover handy, as they will pop like popcorn. Be careful not to burn the seeds, or they will impart a bitter taste to the dish. For a tasty cocktail snack, toss toasted pumpkin seeds with a little oil, salt, and chili powder, spread on a cookie sheet, and bake at 350 degrees for 10 to 12 minutes.

## Tomatillos

Although tomatillos are often referred to as "green tomatoes," they are actually members of the gooseberry family. To prepare tomatillos for most recipes, remove their papery husks and rinse away their sticky outer coating. Place them in a nonreactive pot, add cold water to cover, and bring to a boil. Cook about 8 to 10 minutes, or until the tomatillos soften and the green color fades. For roasted tomatillos, use tongs to place them on a hot comal, turning often until the outer skins blister. Fresh tomatillos will vary in flavor, and it may sometimes be necessary to add a little sugar to sauces to balance their acidic tartness. Canned whole tomatillos are also available. (San Marcos brand)

## Tomatoes

Native to the New World, tomatoes are an important ingredient in many Mexican dishes and are prepared in a variety of ways. For recipes that call for peeled tomatoes, bring a pot of water to a boil, cut an X in the bottom of each tomato, and gently slide them into the boiling water. Boil for up to 1 minute and transfer to a colander. When the tomatoes are cool enough to handle, gently peel away the skin and discard it.

Roasting can be done under a broiler or on a comal, but the broiler is faster and creates less mess. Place tomatoes on a rimmed baking sheet and broil directly under the heat source for 3 minutes. Using tongs, turn tomatoes and broil an additional 3 minutes, or until the tomatoes are blistered all over. Remove from the heat and peel or not, according to the recipe.

## Vanilla Beans and Extract

Along with chocolate and corn, vanilla is one of the New World's great culinary gifts. The international vanilla trade originated from the Mexican port of Veracruz in the late sixteenth century; beans were harvested by native peoples in the rain forests around Papantla. The finest vanilla beans and extract for Mexican cooking still come from that area. (La Vencedora brand extract)

# Basic Equipment

Although many of the recipes may be labor intensive, the preparation of Mexican cuisine does not require lots of expensive, specialized equipment. There are, however, a few tools that will help you reproduce your favorite Fonda dishes in the home kitchen. Some tools, such as the comal and *molcajete*, have been used in Mexico for centuries. Others, such as the *tortillera* and the *molinillo*, are delightfully low-tech and will add Mexican flair to your kitchen equipment. Many of these items are available in good-quality kitchen shops and Hispanic markets or by mail (see "Mail Order Sources").

## Cast-Iron Skillet

A deep, heavy, cast-iron skillet is useful for frying sauces, chiles, and tortillas for enchiladas.

## Chocolate Pot and Molinillo

A decorative ceramic pitcher and wooden, hand-carved stirring stick are the classic tools for preparing Mexican Hot Chocolate.

## Coffee/Spice Grinder

An electric or hand-operated grinder specifically designated for spices, seeds, and nuts is a good idea.

## Comal

This flat metal griddle is placed over a direct flame and used for cooking both corn and flour tortillas as well as toasting other ingredients, such as seeds, nuts, and vegetables for sauces. Comales come in all sizes and shapes, so it is important to choose one that is right for your stove top. Season it lightly with vegetable oil and be sure to dry it thoroughly before storing it to prevent rust.

## Dutch Oven

A large cast-iron or enameled cast-iron Dutch oven will come in handy for preparing moles and *pipianes*.

## Electric Blender

The majority of the sauce recipes call for the use of a blender rather than a food processor because the two appliances render different results. A good-quality home appliance with a heavy-duty motor and removable jar will be a big asset.

## Metal Tongs

Restaurant supply stores carry very affordable metal tongs in a variety of sizes. They are useful when roasting peppers over an open flame, removing toasted items from the comal, and frying tortillas in oil for enchiladas.

## Molcajete

For thousands of years Mexican cooks have been grinding seeds, nuts, and vegetables for sauces in this mortar and pestle, made of dark volcanic rock. *Molcajetes* come in various sizes and consist of a bowl on three legs with a grinding tool. A *molcajete* is particularly handy for grinding small amounts of nuts and seeds or sauces that need to retain a chunky consistency.

## Rubber Gloves

The capsaicin in chiles can burn the skin for hours. Keep good-quality, thin rubber gloves available for handling fresh and dried chiles and chile seeds.

## Stand Mixer

This dependable appliance is by no means a requirement, but having a stand mixer with a paddle attachment, plus all the grinding and sausage-filling attachments, is certainly a plus.

## Tamalera

Although the *tamalera* is specifically designed for steaming tamales, any two-part steamer with a removable basket or rack can be used.

## Tortillera

Once you have eaten freshly made corn tortillas, the nominal cost of a heavy-duty, 6-inch metal tortilla press will seem like a worthwhile investment. To prevent rust, make sure the press is always clean and dry before storing it.

# Mail Order Sources and Recommended Restaurants

When we wrote the first edition of this book, Mexican ingredients were more difficult to find. Happily, much has changed since then. Many chiles, beans, corn, spices and herbs are now available in area markets. In Texas, stores such as HEB, Central Market, Fiesta Mart, and Whole Foods are good places to find ingredients. If you live outside of Texas, California, Arizona, and New Mexico, the following sources are a good place to start. There are many more. We have limited this section to those with which we have firsthand experience.

## Chiles, Corn, and Heirloom Beans

Burns Farm
16158 Hillside Circle
Montverde, FL 34756
(407) 469-4490
www.burnshuitlacoche.com

Épices de cru
C-11, 7070 Avenue Henri Julien
Montréal, QC H2R 2W1 Canada
+1 (514) 273-1118
http://epicesdecru.com

Imagine our surprise when we stumbled on this terrific source. They often have some of the most difficult-to-find dried chiles from Mexico.

Masienda
info@masienda.com

A purveyor of Mexican landrace corn, Masienda supports smallholder farmers in Mexico with non-GMO corn, chiles, and beans. They are supplying many of the most authentic Mexican restaurants.

Purcell Mountain Farms
393 Firehouse Road
Moyie Springs, ID 83845
(208) 267-0627
www.purcellmountainfarms.com

We purchase white and blue dry corn from Purcell for our masa items.

Rancho Gordo
1924 Yajome Street
Napa, CA 94539
(707) 259-1935
www.ranchogordo.com

They also have artisanal Oaxacan chocolate and banana vinegar, as well as other items not generally found— just ask.

## Huitlacoche

Fresh and fresh frozen (at one time, never available except in canned form), this Mexican "truffle" or mushroom, a real delicacy, is known by traditional Mexican chefs and restaurants but is also increasingly found on non-Mexican restaurant menus. The best, perhaps only source, in the United States is:

## General Mexican Food Products

Melissa Guerra Company
303 Pearl Parkway, Suite 104
San Antonio, TX 78215
(877) 875-2665
www.melissaguerra.com

Inquire about whatever you may be seeking in Mexican food products and it is likely they will have it, including Mexican cooking equipment and utensils.

## Recommended Restaurants

There are many authentic Mexican restaurants throughout the United States now, which is a wonderful development. This is a limited but, we think, very good list of traditional Mexican restaurants. We include only those where we have dined.

Cala
149 Fell Street
San Francisco, CA 94102
(415) 660-7701
www.calarestaurant.com

Caracol
2200 Post Oak Boulevard, Suite 160
Houston, TX 77056
(713) 622-9996
http://caracol.net

Cosme
35 East 21st Street
New York, NY 10010
(212) 913-9659
http://cosmenyc.com/

Fonda (there are three)
  Chelsea
  189 9th Avenue
  New York, NY 10011
  (917) 525-5252

  East Village
  40 Avenue B
  New York, NY 10009
  (212) 677-4096

  Park Slope
  434 7th Avenue
  Brooklyn, NY 11215
  (718) 369-3144
  http://fondarestaurant.com/

Frontera Grill, Topolobampo, and Xoco
445 North Clark Street
Chicago, IL 60654
(312) 661-1434
rickbayless.com

Guelaguetza
3014 West Olympic Boulevard
Los Angeles, CA 90006
(213) 427-0608
www.ilovemole.com

Hugo's
1600 Westheimer Road
Houston, TX 77006
(713) 524-7744
http://hugosrestaurant.net/

Lula's Cocina Mexicana
2720 Main Street
Santa Monica, CA 90405
(310) 392-5711
http://lulacocinamexicana.com/index.html

Salpicon
1252 North Wells Street
Chicago, IL 60610
(312) 988-7811
http://salpicon.com/

Gray Hawn

*A good friend in Austin, Gray is known worldwide for her exquisite photography. This was taken by Gray under a bridge in Cuernavaca, and shows mariachis at rest with incredible graffiti in the background. It was included in her exhibit* Romancing Mexico.

Bob "Daddy-O" Wade

*A vintage photo (circa 1940–1950), likely taken in Monterrey, Mexico, enhanced in Bob's unique style.*

## María de los Angeles Pedrosa

*Niña*, 1977.
Oil on canvas, 20 × 14 inches.

*For a few years, the Fonda San Miguel staff made annual trips together to different places in Mexico. This small but adorable painting is a "souvenir" from a group trip to Guanajuato in 1977. Purchased at Sylvia Samuelson's Galería San Miguel in San Miguel de Allende, the painting usually hangs near the restaurant's host stand. As patrons arrive, they invariably smile when they catch sight of the little girl's gleeful expression.*

*T.G.*

# FONDA SAN MIGUEL
## Forty Years of Food and Art

TOM GILLILAND is a graduate of the University of Nebraska and the Law School of the University of Texas at Austin. He also studied law at the Universidad National Autónoma de México in Mexico City as well as at the American Institute of Foreign Trade (now the Garvin School of International Management) in Glendale, Arizona. A co-founder of two restaurants, San Angel Inn in Houston and Fonda San Miguel in Austin, he is an active member of the International Association of Culinary Professionals and a generous supporter of many Austin organizations. At the Fonda San Miguel, Tom has hired the "front of the house" staff for many years and directs the interior design and art collection.

MIGUEL RAVAGO first learned to cook from his grandmother, a native of Sonora, Mexico. A co-founder of San Angel Inn and Fonda San Miguel, he has been a pioneer of regional Mexican cooking for more than thirty years. Miguel co-authored *Cocina de la Familia* with Marilyn Tausend in 1997, which won a Julia Child cookbook award in 1998 and has also been published in Spanish. He is a longtime member of the International Association of Culinary Professionals.

VIRGINIA B. WOOD, a native Texan and a graduate of the University of Texas at Austin, began her professional cooking career as the first pastry chef at Fonda San Miguel restaurant in 1977. She went on to operate her own wholesale dessert and catering company for many years before becoming a food journalist. She is now the food editor at the *Austin Chronicle* and is also a member of the International Association of Culinary Professionals and the Southern Foodways Alliance.

FOOD PHOTOGRAPHY: Tracey Maurer, assisted by Kathie Garcia

FOOD STYLING: Julie Hettiger

Additional food styling by Alicia Mendez-Clayton: pages 152 and 191

PROP STYLING: Jan B. Bailey

ART AND ARCHITECTURE PHOTOGRAPHY:
Paul Bardagjy, Tracy Maurer, various interiors and art objects

Additional interior and personnel photography by Tracey Maurer: endpapers, pages 14, 29, 32, 38, 56, 138, 155, 212, 216, 217, and 221. Photos on pages 42, 127, and 227 by Charles Quinn.

CULINARY CONSULTANT: Cristina Potters